FAITH

Praise for the series:

It was only a matter of time before a clever publisher realized that there is an audience for whom *Exile on Main Street* or *Electric Ladyland* are as significant and worthy of study as *The Catcher in the Rye* or *Middlemarch* . . . The series . . . is freewheeling and eclectic, ranging from minute rock-geek analysis to idiosyncratic personal celebration
— *The New York Times Book Review*

Ideal for the rock geek who thinks liner notes just aren't enough
— *Rolling Stone*

One of the coolest publishing imprints on the planet
— *Bookslut*

These are for the insane collectors out there who appreciate fantastic design, well-executed thinking and things that make your house look cool. Each volume in this series takes a seminal album and breaks it down in startling minutiae. We love these. We are huge nerds
— *Vice*

A brilliant series . . . each one a work of real love
— *NME* (UK)

Passionate, obsessive and sm‑ ‑

Reli‡

T0205152

[A] consistently excellent series
— *Uncut* (UK)

We . . . aren't naive enough to think that we're your only source for reading about music (but if we had our way . . . watch out). For those of you who really like to know everything there is to know about an album, you'd do well to check out Bloomsbury's '33 1/3' series of books
— *Pitchfork*

For reviews of individual titles in the series, please visit our blog at 333sound.com and our website at http://www.bloomsbury. com/musicandsoundstudies
Follow us on Twitter: @333books

Like us on Facebook: https://www.facebook.com/33.3books

For a complete list of books in this series, see the back of this book.

Forthcoming in the series:

Blackout by Natasha Lasky
I Want You by Derrais Carter
That's the Way of the World by Dwight E. Brooks
Fontanelle by Selena Chambers
Come to My Garden by Brittnay L. Proctor
Nightbirds by Craig Seymour
Come Away with ESG by Cheri Percy
Time's Up by Kimberly Mack
BBC Radiophonic Workshop – A Retrospective by William Weir
Madvillainy by Will Hagle
Beauty and the Beat by Lisa Whittington-Hill
and many more . . .

Faith

Matthew Horton

BLOOMSBURY ACADEMIC
NEW YORK • LONDON • OXFORD • NEW DELHI • SYDNEY

BLOOMSBURY ACADEMIC
Bloomsbury Publishing Inc
1385 Broadway, New York, NY 10018, USA
50 Bedford Square, London, WC1B 3DP, UK
29 Earlsfort Terrace, Dublin 2, Ireland

BLOOMSBURY, BLOOMSBURY ACADEMIC and the Diana logo are trademarks of
Bloomsbury Publishing Plc

First published in the United States of America 2022

Library of Congress Cataloging-in-Publication Data
Names: Horton, Matthew, author.
Title: Faith / Matthew Horton.
Description: [1st.] | New York : Bloomsbury Academic, 2022. | Series: 33 1/3 |
Includes bibliographical references. | Summary: On Saturday 28 June 1986, George
Michael picked up his tasselled leather jacket, walked out of London's Wembley Stadium
and cheerfully tore up five years of glittering pop history. He'd just disposed of Wham!,
the band he'd formed with school friend Andrew Ridgeley when they were teenagers,
and now, at 23, he knew he was all grown up. He just needed to convince everyone else.
Faith is what happens when you've outstripped your dreams, your peers, your friends and
your fans, and no one's caught up yet. It's about pouring all of that confusion, insecurity
and sizzling ambition into music that comes out confused, insecure and ambitious – and
then selling 25 million copies of it. George Michael was always preparing for this and, in
the process, he set a template for all disaffected singers making that move. This book
examines that model and the themes that went into Faith – from engaging in politics to
crossing over to the black audience and writing classic pop songs to endure – and speaks
to the surviving key players to tell the story of how it was made
Provided by publisher. Identifiers: LCCN 2021052923 (print) | LCCN 2021052924 (ebook) |
ISBN 9781501377976 (paperback) | ISBN 9781501377983 (epub) |
ISBN 9781501377990 (pdf) | ISBN 9781501378003
Subjects: LCSH: Michael, George, 1963–2016. Faith. |
Michael, George, 1963–2016–Criticism and interpretation. |
Popular music–1981–1990–History and criticism.
Classification: LCC ML410.M644 H67 2022 (print) |
LCC ML410.M644 (ebook) | DDC 782.42166092–dc23
LC record available at https://lccn.loc.gov/2021052923
LC ebook record available at https://lccn.loc.gov/2021052924

ISBN: PB: 978-1-5013-7797-6
ePDF: 978-1-5013-7799-0
eBook: 978-1-5013-7798-3

Series: 33 1/3

Typeset by Newgen KnowledgeWorks Pvt. Lt., Chennai, India
Printed and bound in the United States of America

To find out more about our authors and books visit www.bloomsbury.com
and sign up for our newsletters.

Contents

Track listing   vi
Acknowledgements   vii

Wham! wrapped   1
The public image   7
Freedom 87   23
Sex and the serious man   37
Politics (the pop remix)   53
I will be your adult contemporary   69
Bearing the crossover   91
Signing off   111

Notes   117
Selected bibliography   125

Track listing

Faith (3:16)
Father Figure (5:36)
I Want Your Sex (Parts I & II) (9:17)
One More Try (5:51)
Hard Day (4:48)
Hand to Mouth (4:36)
Look at Your Hands (4:38)
Monkey (5:06)
Kissing a Fool (4:36)

Acknowledgements

I'm grateful for fascinating and generous interviews with Chris Porter, Rob Kahane, Rob O'Connor (who also supplied the original cover image), Shirley Lewis, Paul Gomersall, Chris Cameron, Paul Gambaccini, Andy Duncan, Roddy Matthews, John Altman, Steve Sidwell and Danny Schogger; for connections made by Sharon Hanley, Louis Barfe, Leah Kardos and Liz Tray; for invaluable editorial advice from Emily Mackay and for time allowed by Tricia Scott. But all my love and the rest of my thanks go to my wife Lisa and daughters Georgia, Abigail and Elodie for their unfailing support and insistence on playing George Michael songs every time it looked like I was procrastinating.

Wham! wrapped

After five hectic years stuffed with number one singles, shuttlecocks and timeless songs, British pop duo Wham! were on the verge of a carefully orchestrated split. Their final gig – astutely billed as *The Final*, to take place at London's Wembley Stadium on 28 June 1986 – would free 23-year-old singer George Michael from the tender ministrations and mimed guitar riffs of colleague Andrew Ridgeley and set him on the path to inevitable solo stardom. He had to be happy about that, right? 'I'm making a single with Aretha Franklin', he told effervescent British pop magazine *Smash Hits* a month beforehand, 'and possibly one in June with Michael Jackson. With opportunities to work with people like that how can you *not* be happy?'[1] Michael's status was getting an upgrade and his status anxiety with it.

Thirty years later, following his death on Christmas Day 2016, stories emerged of Michael's boundless, secret generosity, of millions given to worthy recipients over the years without a whiff of publicity, from the nurses of the UK's National Health Service to celebrities lolloping across the English Channel.[2] He was used to keeping some things private, dodging questions about his sexuality for the best part of two decades in the limelight. But for a man so caught up in his image and what the public thought of him, it was strange to find such a bright spot concealed. Perhaps he was finally comfortable in his own skin. Not like in the old days: while Wham! were racking up the hits at home and abroad in the mid-1980s, delighting everyone with instant classic cuts, Michael was enjoying the trappings of pop fame and the flowering of his talent, but was increasingly frustrated that few could see past the shiny teeth and the Princess Di hair to the serious artist beneath.

There were breakthroughs: 'Careless Whisper', a ballad he and Ridgeley had co-written when they were seventeen, arrived four years later as a solo single in the UK and a 'Wham! featuring George Michael' release in the United States, topping their respective charts and serving notice of Michael's range of skills; 'A Different Corner' in 1986 was an unmitigated solo release, a stark soul-barer that severed the sonic connection between Michael and Wham! a few months before the split became definitive. Breakthroughs, yes, but only because they showed Michael could exploit a handy sideline as a classy white soul singer when the big, brash Wham! hits became too rote. The pair even scoffed at the idea that solo singles meant a fully fledged solo career, giving short shrift to *Smash Hits* journalist Ian Birch when he shared a rumour that Wham!'s then-label Innervision was hatching a scheme to ditch Ridgeley and turn Michael into the star he so obviously was. 'Where did you hear that?' asked Michael. 'If I was left to my own devices, I'd probably try and sound like Marvin Gaye for the next five years. But the important thing is that together we make a pop group.'[3]

A denial that reads like a long-term forecast. Together they made a pop group, but there were things Michael would far rather be doing if he had the space. Slowly but surely, he was fashioning that chance.

As Ridgeley became more and more marginalized and apparently content with his lot – as he revealed in his autobiography *Wham! George & Me*, even before the release of their 1983 debut album *Fantastic* 'we'd decided that Wham!'s creative reins should rest solely with George'[4] – Michael could assert his plan to let Wham! go out on a high, with a vapour trail of unerring number one singles, a big gig for a last tearful embrace with the fans and no loss of face for his old buddy. The practical business was in place; now came the hard bit. Becoming the new George Michael and selling him.

Having taken Wham! as far as they could go – or at least as far as he was prepared to take them – he naturally had to aim higher. Otherwise, what was the point? 'I can now play about with my success to a large degree,' he told *Smash Hits*' Peter Martin as Wham! split. 'I've got two audiences that are both prepared to accept me and so I've more or less got a free rein.'[5] Actually, he was more focused than that. He was after the crown. In 1986, that was a triple crown in the popular consciousness split between Madonna, Prince and Michael Jackson, and, whatever pure pop juice he shared with Madonna, he would forever be pitted against the men.

Realignment was handled by measures. There was 'I Knew You Were Waiting (For Me)', the charmingly cliché-driven transatlantic number one duet released in early 1987 with a slightly detached Aretha Franklin ('She just seemed unimpressed by everything'[6]), which at least showed that Michael could mix it with the best and gained him deeper, desired access to Black audiences – but it stood alone. Giving an insight into the pace of late 1980s pop, the merest period of silence in the months that followed suggested inertia, even utter creative bankruptcy to the fans and the media. Letting a shaft of light fall on his own grudges, former Wham! manager Simon Napier-Bell expressed his horror to *Q* magazine in April 1987: 'George hasn't done a thing without Andrew. He's at number one with Aretha Franklin, but that record was done a year ago. You never know what's propping somebody up.'[7] Napier-Bell's wishful thinking faded into history on 18 May 1987, when Michael unleashed 'I Want Your Sex' and switched the narrative irrevocably.

****

Released on 30 October 1987, George Michael's debut solo album *Faith* is about the establishment of identity, about throwing off the yoke of expectation and planting your own flag in your own soil. You'd think you wouldn't need to claim your own soil, but what if your public doesn't know it's yours? What if they think your soil's over there with the 'screaming kids'?[8] *Faith* is suffused with impostor syndrome.

George Michael wasn't the first singer in a pop band to go solo, he certainly won't be the last, but he may well be the most hung up about it. Let's explore those frustrations, how he got to that point and what he did about it, emotionally, artistically and commercially. We'll watch him grabbing the tiller of his career, fixing his image and mastering the studio. We'll find him brazen in his lyrics even as he cowers in his treasured leather jacket on the album sleeve. We'll see him engaging in politics, where he'd been stung before, then uniting extremes as a paragon of the Adult Contemporary songbook and a genuine crossover sensation. Above all, we'll be able to chart the rise of Georgios Kyriacos Panayiotou, the North West London son of a Cypriot immigrant, from none-more-pop squeaky clean icon to classic songwriter. He made it look easy. We'll see how hard it was.

Faith is a guide book. It is, somewhat self-evidently, the story of how you 'do a George Michael': how you implement a smooth transition from superstar lead singer in a band to superstar solo artist in your own right. Nail it and you're Robbie Williams – albeit taking the overtly literal path of covering 'Freedom', an actual George Michael song, to kick off your solo career. Learn directly from the master and you're Geri Halliwell – briefly matching the commercial feats of the band that birthed you before drawing back. Bungle it and you're Gary Barlow – thinking the prosaic fact that you're switching from band singer-songwriter to solo singer-songwriter is enough. You need a bit more than that. If *Faith* has a handful of prominent themes, one of them is surely control. Throughout the life cycle of Wham!, Michael had gradually been wresting it away from producers, managers, parents and friends, and at last all decisions were down to him, no other human points of failure in the process. He was going to do it, and do it right.

The public image

'George asked us to draw the symbols for the album cover,' remembers Rob O'Connor, creative director of graphic design agency Stylorouge. 'He said they had to represent faith, music, money, religion and love.' He sighs. 'We must have attempted them 20 times.' O'Connor was no stranger to George Michael's perfectionist streak, but this was ridiculous even by the singer's notoriously pernickety standards. 'Finally, he came in one day with a little piece of black paper, and he'd painted them himself in gold. "This is what I had in mind," he said. "Can you follow this?" And I said, "Why follow it? Let's just save everyone a load of time and use these, because you like them." By that time, I knew what he was about.'

Frankly, it's a surprise Michael didn't want to paint the symbols himself in the first place. His grip on the project had to be absolute, from the content to the look. The singer's erstwhile friend and media inside man, writer and broadcaster Paul Gambaccini says, *Faith* is 'both a posture and the complete truth. Emotionally, it's the complete truth, but in terms of videos and imagery, it's a posture. However, that posture is to achieve a goal, which is to be taken seriously as an emotive adult artist.' Get the image right and the rest will follow.

Sometimes image is just that – the right picture, the right framing, the right idea. Trust was important to George Michael, and in O'Connor and Stylorouge, he had a team that had come up with the goods before. 'I first met George in 1982 when Wham! were signed to Innervision, a little label based in Soho,' says O'Connor. 'Innervision approached us to do the cover for Wham!'s June 1982 debut single "Wham Rap! (Enjoy What You Do)", a simple bit of graphic design and a logo, and then we went on to do "Young Guns (Go For It)" and "Bad Boys." The *Fantastic* album came out after that [July 1983] and for some reason they used an almost identical picture to "Bad Boys" – but they didn't bother coming to us for the artwork for that one.' No hard feelings, at least once Innervision were out of the frame.

As far back as the 'Wham Rap!' job, O'Connor had a handle on what the young Michael (then just eighteen) was made of. 'He was quite a hands-on chap', he says with a palpable sense of understatement. When preparations for third single 'Bad Boys' came around in spring 1983, Michael's laser focus appeared even more direct. 'I just found it remarkable,' continues O'Connor, 'the sense of control that he wanted over his life and career. He was very respectful of what people did, but he didn't mind saying if he disliked the results.' There was a photo shoot for 'Bad Boys' with the photographer Eric Watson, then a chief snapper for pre-teen UK pop bible *Smash Hits* and later the go-to video director for the equally divine synth duo Pet Shop Boys (featuring Neil Tennant, former deputy editor of *Smash Hits*). However, the project hadn't started with him. 'We ended up doing three different images for "Bad Boys", but the first two fell on bad luck,' says O'Connor with a dab of irony. 'We set up a shoot one night in Soho with George and Andrew running through the streets, and there were some reasonable shots there, but George didn't like any of them. "I've got another idea," he said. "I'm getting into this biker look and I'd rather do some shots with Eric Watson," who he'd worked with on *Smash Hits* features. So, we went to Eric's studio, where he'd brought in a motorbike, shot a few Polaroids and George was looking at them going, "Nah, nah …" and then getting up and moving boiling hot tungsten lamps around to arrange the shoot the way he wanted. That's when I realized the person I was dealing with.'

The shoot was a salutary experience for everyone, and there were even more valuable lessons to learn. When Michael picked up the proofs from Watson and took them over to Stylorouge, he managed to leave the whole lot in the cab. 'He got out at my office,' continues O'Connor, 'came up the stairs, shouted out, "Shit! Fuck!" and went back down to try and grab the cab. It was gone. So that was awkward. Someone somewhere has a rare Wham! photo shoot and all I ended up with were three or four prints that Eric [Watson] managed to hold onto. After all that, we ended up going with the press shots of the two guys wearing leather jackets, with nothing underneath.' A strong image that would have its day again when Michael reappeared as a be-leathered early 1960s death-disc anti-hero, like he'd stepped straight out of the Shangri-Las' 'Leader of the Pack', for the *Faith* campaign. 'That was the look!' remembers O'Connor. 'And why on earth I didn't realize then that George was gay, I've no idea. It wasn't important, but it never even occurred to me.'

It would be more than four years before Michael and Stylorouge worked together again. Once the campaign for their second album, *Make It Big*, got going in May 1984 with the release of 'Wake Me Up Before You Go-Go', Wham! and George Michael sleeve designs were largely taken care of by Peter Saville Associates who – the rather garish 'Wake Me Up' cover aside – brought some of their minimal Factory aesthetic to prime chart-topping pop. Seen through the Saville prism, the UK cover image of Michael's 'Careless Whisper' is suddenly an obvious relation to the sleeve of Joy Division's *Closer* – and indeed, defying all expectation, Michael revealed it was one of his favourite albums on BBC Two music discussion programme *Eight Days a Week* on 25 May 1984, just as 'Wake Me Up' was crashing into the UK singles chart at number four.

The unlikely dream partnership produced ever more sparse results. On 'A Different Corner', Michael's second UK solo single released in March 1986, the distant figure walking through a snow-specked park is actually Saville himself standing in for Michael;[1] on the UK's final two Wham! singles – 'I'm Your Man' in November 1985 and 'The Edge of Heaven' EP in June 1986 – Michael and Andrew Ridgeley are nowhere to be seen until you open the latter's gatefold sleeve. If Michael was enjoying his habitual creative control, it was clear he was hiding. If he was embarrassed at still being in Wham!, the point was subtly pressed home. Even within that farewell gatefold, Michael was demurely looking away as Ridgeley faced the camera.

The final sleeve Saville made with Michael was coyer still, this time suggestively so. James Wedge's photograph of the bulging, monochrome satin sheets on the cover of 'I Want Your Sex' (released 18 May 1987 in the United States; 1 June in the UK) implies plenty, but the most innocent inference is that the now officially solo Michael remains unready to fully reveal himself to the world. Either that, or he was keeping his face off the cover as a show of strength. Observing from the outside, O'Connor was impressed. 'I thought that worked really well. He liked that touch of sophistication, and the fact he got away with not being on the cover was also very important. That was a real watershed moment for his relationship with the record company, because he dug his heels in and said, "No, I don't want to be on there."'

He was just as bullish when he and O'Connor began work on the *Faith* cover, initially having his name removed – and that's how the first copies of the LP went out, just Michael baring his chest but shielding his million-dollar face with his leather jacket, a sticker added for compromise – and sticking to his guns with the photo he chose. 'There were some people at [Michael's record label, owners of the Epic imprint] CBS who didn't want that picture on *Faith*,' says O'Connor, 'and they certainly didn't want it going out without his name on it. But he won that battle.' It's obvious Michael had an established vision of what the *Faith* package was going to look like, and design agencies, photographers and video directors were the tools to realize it. 'He just wanted me to do a nice, tidy job of visualizing his ideas,' concedes O'Connor. 'Even the photoshoot, he arranged that himself with [photographer] Russell Young. He had a couple of shoots booked: one was with Matthew Rolston of *Rolling Stone*, the other with Russell. He told me about the one with Matthew – which I turned up at – but he didn't mention the one with Russell, the shoot that produced the cover photo.'

The secrecy was appropriate to the result. Naturally, critics had fun with the pose. 'Why is George sniffing his armpit on the cover?' asked *Melody Maker*'s Steve Sutherland in a scornful review. 'Could it be a visual symbol of the album's intended carnality? Or could it just be that the album stinks?'[2] O'Connor, thankfully, has a more considered take. 'He wanted something really intimate, very up close and personal. I remember thinking at the time that it was a remarkably good picture – everything was thought through, from the little earring to the attitude. It looked as if he was sharing a secret with someone.' O'Connor thinks the photo expresses the mood of the album. 'It looked like the album sounded – to me. His voice is very breathy on the record and the music is a club production, so it's as if he's in a corridor behind a club, sharing a moment.' That said, it also conveys that new-found diffidence. As Michael himself told the *Chicago Tribune* a year after *Faith*'s release, 'I swear, if I never have to stand in front of a camera again I'd be happy.'[3] He'd follow through on that plan when second album *Listen Without Prejudice Vol. 1* came around.

O'Connor enjoyed the simplicity of the artwork from a practical perspective, happy to avoid making infinitesimal changes with a scalpel and Spray Mount in the middle of the night. Michael had even wanted the cover to be monochrome originally, but they saved that concept for the single sleeve of skeletal, hip-swinging rock 'n' roll pastiche 'Faith', enhanced with a touch of blue to the eyes ('I resisted that,' says O'Connor, 'but he got his way, of course.') Inevitably, the singer had firm views on the *Faith* typeface. 'He wanted it to look like Chanel. It was part of the Helvetica family, or Grotesque, a sans serif font. Once he'd mentioned Chanel, we looked at some packaging and matched that. It was very straightforward – the singles were the same.' Straightforward as far as the labour was concerned; less so when it came to thrashing it out with the suits.

'George wanted the sleeve for "Father Figure" [*Faith*'s astonishing, gospel-flavoured third UK single – and fourth US, after the club issue of 'Hard Day' – released on 28 December 1987] to be pure white, but the record company wasn't happy and insisted we have a picture. So, he and I messed around with just how transparent you can go before an image disappears, using layers of tracing paper over prints to see how it would look. The label finally compromised and went for this washed-out, blue-grey colour.' A small victory taken care of. Subsequent sleeves went the whole hog – 'One More Try', 'Kissing a Fool' and 'Monkey' just pristine titles on plain backgrounds. As the *Faith* campaign wore on, George Michael was fading away before our very eyes.

He was a mere twinkle in a record company executive's eye when Paul Gambaccini first heard of him. At a wedding reception early in 1982 at Hogarth's House, Chiswick Park, Innervision Records manager Mark Dean came bounding up with some exciting news – for Dean at least. 'He said, "I've just signed these two boys. You're going to love them." ' The unfortunate Dean was history by the time Gambaccini actually met Michael in the flesh, in the salubrious surroundings of the Solihull Conference and Banqueting Centre, a little way off an M1 motorway interchange in the West Midlands. The event was the Marathon Music Quiz, an annual charity bash, by 1984 held in association with IPC's *No.1* magazine, the hopeful rival to EMAP's pop mag market leader *Smash Hits*, with Gambaccini a team captain as usual. 'The quiz would halt every hour for a five-minute comfort break, and during one of those I went backstage and – spotting someone out of the corner of my eye – I thought, "Who's that sad gay boy? Oh, that's George Michael." I didn't think anything more about it, just wrote it off as me projecting.'

Sidelining those assumptions, Gambaccini became friends with Michael with an ease that drew from his lengthy experience in radio and the barriers broken down when you were a music man rather than a celebrity DJ. In the mid-1980s there were plenty of the latter on Radio 1, a cadre of hairstyles using their slot on the airwaves and the *Top of the Pops* gig that came with it to reap personal appearance fees and further TV careers. Gambaccini, however, was one of the old-school breed notable for their passion for music – although a few TV talking head spots couldn't harm anything. 'I probably interviewed George more than anyone else because I didn't have a big-game hunter approach to it. And of course, I also got to know the people of his inner circle – his sister Melanie, David Austin, [his plugger] Gary Farrow.' Gambaccini was still the go-to man for interviews as late as Michael's *Symphonica* tour, a quasi-warm-up man hosting the introductory press conference and chat with the singer on 11 May 2011 at London's Royal Opera House.

As an intimate, Gambaccini picked up discreet insights, and one stood out as a glimpse into Michael's mindset on going solo. At dinner with Michael, Farrow and Elton John at venerable French restaurant L'Escargot in London's Soho in the early 1990s, Gambaccini heard a surprising take. 'George turned to Elton and said, "I really envy you guys from the 1970s – you had each other to bounce off. I'm on my own." He was referring to Elton and Rod [Stewart] and [David] Bowie, all of them working at the same time.' Michael explicitly aired these thoughts in an interview with the *New York Times* in September 1990, saying, 'I've grown up in a period where … all you have to do to have ever-increasing fame is to repeat what has been successful before.' In the glory days of the 1970s, 'those people all had a desperate desire to move ahead of each other'.[4] Not that Michael was prolific like his antecedents – anything but. Yet some of his peers were. Prince, for instance, at the time of *Faith*, was releasing albums as frequently as anyone had ever done, albeit in splendid isolation. Michael Jackson was operating more on Michael's timetable, although he was hardly a sparring partner one could ring up and bounce ideas off. In the UK, where Michael might have had his Bowie, he could swing between the extremes of Rick Astley and Phil Collins, neither likely to excite his creative juices. Astley was no writer, even if as a singer he moved in the same vaguely sophisticated pop arena (and would achieve the improbable feat of knocking Michael off the Hot 100 number one spot twice in 1988; first in March, ousting 'Father Figure' with 'Never Gonna Give You Up', and then in June, 'Together Forever' dethroning 'One More Try'), while Collins was no critical darling, despite the vast shipments of units. The likes of Bowie, Stewart and John remained in the frame at a rarefied level, complacency or ill-advised audacity betraying careers that had lost their natural forward thrust. Perhaps his nearest British kin was Mick Hucknall of Simply Red. Flanking 1990's *Listen Without Prejudice Vol. 1*, the 1989 album *A New Flame* and 1991 follow-up *Stars* represented the brief, dizzyingly successful flowering of Hucknall's talent before his own impetus began to dissipate. Their peaks never quite met. Figuratively, at least from his own vantage point, Michael was out there alone.

For all their professional – and a certain amount of personal – closeness, and whatever the Professor of Pop's intuition was picking up, Michael had never confided in Gambaccini that he was gay. 'Looking back, it was kind of ridiculous,' he says now, 'because I was out. If George had wanted to confide in anyone in the business, surely it should have been either myself or Freddie [Mercury] or Boy George?' Boy George was regularly trying to 'out' Michael to the press – in his notoriously waspish style ('I love George Michael and I think he's extremely talented,' he told *Smash Hits* in 1987, 'I just said he lived in a cupboard.'[5]) – so might not have been the best choice of a sounding board. In any case, Michael was nowhere near talking to anyone in the LGBTQ+ community; he was barely ready to talk to the mirror. 'I know for a while he was trying to deny it to himself,' says Gambaccini, 'but I also knew if he had a problem he could talk to Melanie or David.' The George Michael inner circle stayed solid throughout his life, and beyond, with only second cousin Andros (or Andreas) Georgiou appearing to break ranks.

Andros Georgiou was the son of Dimitrios 'Jimmy' Georgiou, who emigrated from Cyprus in the 1950s with his own cousin Kyriacos Panayiotou, Michael's father, and was also joint founder of Aegean Records with the singer, co-releasing the majority of Michael's post-*Listen Without Prejudice Vol. 1* recordings as well as putting out the 1997 single 'Waltz Away Dreaming' by Toby Bourke featuring Michael – an elegiac tribute to Michael's late, beloved mother Lesley. Further back, Georgiou had previously recorded as Boogie Box High with Michael again popping up as the thinly disguised singer of 1987 UK top 10 hit 'Jive Talkin''. The links went deep. Tempers flared in 1998 when Georgiou called Michael out for his blasé handling of his arrest in Los Angeles on 7 April for lewd behaviour, and also for his recreational drug use. Georgiou had mentioned to UK gossip magazine *Hello!* that he 'was the only person who went ballistic at [Michael] over the arrest in the spring . . . I can do that with him. Everyone else is scared'.[6] As it happened, apparently Georgiou couldn't do that with him after all, and within a few weeks *The Sun* newspaper was reporting a 'massive bust-up', with the result that 'the cousins have gone their separate ways following the huge row'.[7] In later years Georgiou and his wife Jacqueline would sometimes be seen in the press returning to the subject of Michael's drug issues. That the reports are remarkable at all is testament to how close-knit the circle was. Tragically – if surely a source of contentment later – there seems to have been a rapprochement between the pair immediately before Michael's death.

The confidences kept for the rest of his life were those shared with old friends Austin, Shirlie Holliman (later Kemp, wife of Spandau Ballet bassist Martin) and, of course, Andrew Ridgeley. Not until Ridgeley's memoir *Wham! George & Me*, published in 2019, did his comrade put down in words how Michael had told him and Holliman he was gay, while on the 'Club Tropicana' video shoot in Ibiza in early summer 1983. 'I later learned he'd confided in Shirlie first,' Ridgeley wrote. 'I guess he was looking for assurance from her that I would be OK.'[8] It had taken fifteen years from that confession before the rest of the world was sure; another twenty-one years for Ridgeley to tell the story. That's a watertight team, but Michael had alluded to the moment in his first interview with the gay press, in *The Advocate*, in January 1999. 'I had decided I was really bisexual and told [Ridgeley and Holliman],' he said. 'I told them that I wanted to tell my mum and dad. . . . But they made me think just long enough to back out of it, and I often wonder if things would've been very different.'[9]

Even with Gambaccini, Michael was as guarded about his professional plans as he was about his personal life, refusing to drop hints about a solo move, whatever the mammoth 1984 success of 'Careless Whisper'. Its release in the United States as a 'Wham! featuring George Michael' single dampened speculation, and in the UK it was sandwiched between a couple of Wham! hits in such a carefree manner that it felt more like a spotlight falling on the singer during a gig than any real breakaway. What it did though was make people take notice. 'I was interviewing Ray Parker Jr. [former Raydio frontman and singer of the *Ghostbusters* theme, a *Billboard* Hot 100 number one single in June 1984] in Los Angeles while "Careless Whisper" was number one in America [late February to early March 1985],' says Gambaccini, 'and Ray just shook his head, marvelling at the lyrics. There was a world outside George that was responding to him.'

Gambaccini knows Michael was right to part with Ridgeley because 'Wham! had done its job'. It was blatant in pure *Billboard* terms, because *Make It Big* – Wham!'s second and last album in the UK; second of three (with 1986's *Music from the Edge of Heaven* gathering all the loose ends) in the United States – had scored three Hot 100 number one singles in 'Wake Me Up Before You Go-Go', 'Careless Whisper' and 'Everything She Wants' (the AA-side to 'Last Christmas' in the UK), while *Music from the Edge of Heaven* managed none.

As a pop historian, Gambaccini sees the same scholarly nous in Michael. 'I think he realized that the shelf life of a teen group is four years. The 1970s were his formative decade, so he would have seen that The Osmonds were incredibly popular and then they weren't; The Jackson Five were incredibly popular and then they weren't. George's big idols of the 1970s were Stevie Wonder, The Isley Brothers and Elton John, so he would've seen this only goes so far, but if you're Stevie or Elton it can go on forever. I would've thought he was itching to get out.' Creatively, Wham! were eating themselves too, 'The Edge of Heaven' a bland retread of the more accomplished Motown tribute 'Freedom'. Gambaccini feels Michael was keeping material pent up inside him, 'because each of those five hits off *Faith* are not Wham! singles'. It's as if Michael was his own George Harrison, temporarily stymied by the dominant Wham!-Michael just as Harrison was by The Beatles' semi-benign dictators, before everything came pouring out at the first chance of autonomy. In a superbly awkward interview with British chat show host

Jonathan Ross around the time of 'I Want Your Sex', Michael concurs, pointing out the songs he was writing in the last year or so of Wham! were 'becoming more mature, and also I found it incredibly difficult to write for the group image when I was writing much more personal lyrics'.[10]

How he went about introducing himself as a bona fide solo artist was rather less tsunamic than George Harrison's triple-album splurge. The first single out the door – 'I Knew You Were Waiting (For Me)' – was a Simon Climie and Dennis Morgan co-write, so hardly displaying Michael's own songwriting chops, and he was sharing the limelight with a much bigger star in Aretha Franklin, even though the flow of benefits was inarguably two-way. 'I Knew You Were Waiting (For Me)' didn't appear on *Faith* later that year, because it had done what it set out to do: unlocked a new audience for Franklin and jacked up Michael's soul credibility. 'George obviously didn't think that "I Knew You Were Waiting (For Me)" fit the artistic mood of what he was going to do with *Faith*,' says Gambaccini. Aesthetically admirable, but no way to launch a campaign, and the next single kept things off-piste.

The crotch-led acid funk of 'I Want Your Sex' rushed ahead as the first single of the *Faith* campaign, because it featured on the soundtrack to Eddie Murphy's latest glitzy movie vehicle *Beverly Hills Cop II*, in cinemas from May 1987. Although the third track from the movie to be released as a single, it came out the same week as the theatrical release, clearly deemed to have tie-in cachet – which it then blew by being basically unplayable. Notwithstanding its airplay-repellent lyric and video, 'I Want Your Sex' possibly does *Faith* another disfavour (if one assumes the single's controversy really did hamper it), by giving a false impression. It's not a reliable barometer for *Faith*'s prevailing climate. 'Like "The Girl is Mine" [the October 1982 duet between Paul McCartney and Michael Jackson, which preceded its own parent album, Michael Jackson's *Thriller*, by around eight weeks],' says Gambaccini, 'the first single gives a totally non-indicative sense of what the album's going to be about.' It does, however, serve another, more insidious purpose. 'What it did do,' Gambaccini continues, 'was mark a big dividing line. Andrew [Ridgeley] would never have been raunchy.'

It's a wonder *Faith* became so huge, how those twenty-five million units and counting flooded into homes the world over, when George Michael was inadvertently derailing the hype train. He successfully peeved the radio stations with 'I Want Your Sex', then followed it up with the title track and its 34-second fade-in cathedral organ intro. Gambaccini remembers it being just as much of a treat for DJs: 'It's impossible to talk over because you don't even know if it's started yet! And then you have these ballads that are over five minutes long.'

The ballads were to be expected – part of the George Michael package – seeded by 'Careless Whisper' and 'A Different Corner'. Crudely, the public perception was that Wham! were joy, Michael was gloom. 'The glummest man in pop?' went the headline of *Smash Hits*' profile in November 1987, with the singer conceding, 'I've *always* taken myself seriously. And I always took the pop music I made far more seriously than most people gave me credit for.'[11] The two strands weren't so far apart in his eyes. 'I write MOR ballads which are very successful,' he told *No.1* magazine in June 1986 for Wham!'s final interview together, 'but I also have the advantage of being only 22 years old with a whole market and a whole image that I can play around with. There are musical areas I feel I haven't entered yet.'[12] Within a couple of months he was starting to bat that image around at Sarm (or SARM, Sound and Recording Mobiles) West Studios in Notting Hill, West London, the complex acquired from Island Records by producer Trevor Horn and his wife Jill Sinclair, where their ZTT label oversaw the recording of immense, state-of-the-art albums like (at least some of) Frankie Goes to Hollywood's *Welcome to the Pleasuredome* (1984) and Propaganda's *A Secret Wish* (1985).

Michael and his team set about 'I Want Your Sex' and 'Look at Your Hands' during August and September at Sarm, before the operation moved to the Jutland peninsula and Denmark's Puk Studios in February 1987, then back to Sarm in April – with stop-offs in Paris and at Genesis's Fisher Lane Farm studios in Surrey, south of London – then returning to Puk for May and early June, and finally wrapping up at Sarm from the end of June to the start of October. Just over a year to make the biggest album of his career.

Freedom 87

George Michael is credited as the producer and arranger on *Faith*, the man with the plan and final say. The knobs, though, were twiddled by Chris Porter, the engineer, who also placed the mics, set the delay times and fell off a horse. While Michael had an expanding understanding of what it took to make a record, he was never going to be the guy with the extreme technical know-how, so he needed someone he could trust.

He and Porter went back years, right to the start, although you wouldn't know it. Bookkeeping's never been big in pop. 'Credits on records were always discretionary,' says Andy Duncan, (credited) percussionist on 'Look at Your Hands'. 'No one was obliged to credit anybody for anything if they didn't want to.' The producer of Wham!'s debut single – 'Wham Rap! (Enjoy What You Do)', a non-hit on initial release in June 1982, then top 10 in the UK with its 'Special U.S. Re-Mix' the following January after they'd broken through with 'Young Guns (Go For It)' – was Bob Carter, who, after enjoying some success with the Brit-funk of Linx and Junior, was brought in by Wham!'s label Innervision to see if he could bestow some of that hip authenticity on the new boys. His good friend Chris Porter was in tow.

Search the limited 'Wham Rap!' single credits and the more expansive details on Wham!'s debut album *Fantastic*, released in July 1983, and you'll see no sign of Porter, although Carter gets his due – the rest of the record was produced by the late Steve Brown, veteran of the early 1970s glory years of Michael's childhood hero Elton John. The album was largely recorded at Maison Rouge Studios in Fulham, West London, but again, there were sessions at Good Earth Studios – owned by stellar David Bowie producer Tony Visconti – in Soho, Central London, which Porter engineered without attribution. When Innervision came to prepare the fourth single from *Fantastic* – 'Club Tropicana', released a couple of weeks after the album came out – they found spare material pretty thin on the ground, so booked the band back into Good Earth for a rapid twelve-hour session, locked in like Rumpelstiltskin's straw-spinning future princess until they delivered a B-side. The result was the close, hushed soul of 'Blue (Armed with Love)', early notice of Michael's accelerating songwriting skills. Chris Porter was of course the unlisted engineer, George Michael was – for the first time – the sole producer.

Nevertheless, Porter was now on board for real. By the time Wham! returned after the best part of a year scrapping with Innervision and, eventually, signing up with Epic, he was the official engineer to Michael's all-controlling producer. A credit was still conspicuous by its absence on the comeback single 'Wake Me Up Before You Go-Go' in May 1984 and its follow-up 'Freedom' in October. Porter would have to wait until the second album *Make It Big* a month later to see his name in figurative lights, and after that it came like a flood, the words 'Recorded by Chris Porter' a mainstay of Wham!'s single sleeves to the amicable end.

He hadn't expected quite so much, of anything, at the beginning. 'I can remember the first time I met them,' says Porter now. 'We recorded "Wham Rap!" at RAK Studios [St John's Wood, North London, a strong-armed stone's throw from Abbey Road] and Bob Carter and I had been setting up the rhythm section when George and Andrew came in. They were both wearing extremely skimpy tennis shorts, George had really tight curly hair at the time, and he was a little bit spotty. They were both energetic and fun, but I thought, "I don't know if this has got any legs at all," so when "Wham Rap!" did reasonably well on its second release, my opinion changed a bit.

'Even so, I didn't see George's spark of genius, but I think that's because it was probably only his second or third time in a studio, and he was working with a producer [Carter, who also played keyboards on 'Wham Rap!'] who was very musical, and George was slightly cowed by that. But he knew what he wanted from his vocals even then. He would press to keep redoing bits until he was happy, which is unusual in a callow young artist. They just go, "Thank god for that!" when they're done recording, whereas George would say, "No, I can do that better." '

Once Porter came back into the Wham! fold for 'Blue (Armed with Love)' and then on a more reliable basis for 'Wake Me Up', he grew to understand his new place and George's rising confidence. 'George was always in control of everything he did. I think one of the reasons he moved on from [*Fantastic* producer] Steve Brown was because he wanted more control and I don't think Steve was letting him have it. When we worked together on "Blue", I was very cognizant of both their talents – George and Andrew – and what they were aiming for. I simply gave them the tools to do what they wanted.'

If it all looked like plain sailing for the new recording partnership, it could have been scuppered before they'd even left harbour. Wham!'s manager Simon Napier-Bell had come up with the bright idea of taking the untapped super-weapon in the band's armoury – future George Michael showcase 'Careless Whisper' – to Atlantic production legend Jerry Wexler, who apparently loved the song and suggested they skip over to Alabama in the late summer of 1983 and record it at Muscle Shoals, surely its destiny as a prime slab of yearning soul. 'At that stage, I thought it was all over,' says Porter. 'They've gone over to the States to work with Jerry Wexler who's got a huge reputation and loads of experience. I said to myself, "That's it, I'll probably never see them again."' Contrary to all expectations, the Wexler sessions didn't work out – none of the vastly experienced sax players they auditioned could nail what Michael wanted from the now-celebrated solo, and the whole recording lacked that indefinable something. 'It sounded too much like standard Muscle Shoals product,' Napier-Bell wrote later. 'Slick and correct in the accepted manner, but no more than that either.'[1] Porter was delighted: 'A few weeks afterwards, they came back into the studio and said, "We want to record it all again." It felt good.'

Porter had received fair warning that Wham! were to split, long before *The Final* at Wembley Stadium in June 1986. 'I remember we had the conversation about them splitting at an airport and George said he'd like to continue working with me, and I was obviously very keen because we'd had quite a lot of success by then,' he confirms. 'Andrew [Ridgeley]'s a very affable character and he was relaxed about it all. He'd always known that George was the driving force and was incredibly ambitious at the time. So, he said his goodbyes and George said his new hellos!'

****

In February 1987, with very little in the can so far beside the initial tapes from late summer's Sarm sessions, the whole *Faith* shebang decamped to Puk Recording Studios, near Randers, Denmark, far from the madding crowd. And far from the taxman. 'I guess [it was] for tax purposes,' Michael conceded to British DJ Mark Goodier for the *Faith: Legacy Edition* rerelease in 2011. 'The whole tax year out didn't agree with me at all.'[2] It had been a point of principle to him. 'I'm the only one of that whole band of 1984 stars who hasn't done a year out of the country for tax reasons,'[3] he told *NME*'s Alan Jackson in June 1987. It only became a year out after the *Faith* tour took him away from the UK for so much longer, although it's hard to imagine his accountants springing the exile on him without his knowledge. Mad, maddening, taxing, whichever, it was a crowd driving Michael to distraction, desperate for a piece of one of the biggest pop stars on the planet. 'At Sarm, he just used to get ambushed all the time,' says Porter, 'so we needed a peaceful place to record. A friend of mine, Andy

Munro, had designed Puk Studios, so I was very keen to work there. It just looked amazing in terms of equipment and monitoring. The way that the recording rooms, the control rooms and the booths were arranged seemed ideal for what we wanted to do. We could get all the people in there that we needed – four or five of us at once, all with our own set-ups, all able to work at once. Also, it was a residential studio and very difficult to get to. It was just very attractive.'

Puk's relatively glamorous accoutrements had been assembled with healthy support. 'It had been heavily subsidized by the Danish government. The owners had received some incredible grants for the building and the technology, so it was very well equipped. They had some beautiful mics which they'd bought from Denmark Radio, all the digital machines already on site, the desk we liked – and the rates were very good!'

With its top-notch facilities and hand-picked staff, Puk was an ideal place to spend time getting *Faith* together, now a somewhat alien thought. 'It's very rare nowadays that you get to spend that long making an album, as we did with *Faith*,' Porter says. 'These days, you generally get into a studio for perhaps a couple of weeks to do rhythm tracks and then disappear into your little holes to do overdubs.' It's in stark contrast to the heyday of crafting a classic album. 'It's not as much fun. There's nothing better than being in the studio with a bunch of people, experimenting, being able to comment and revise as you go.' Speaking at the time of the Covid-19 pandemic, enduring its seismic effect on working practices across all industries, Porter feels that lack of direct teamwork even more keenly. 'You can't pounce on those moments of serendipity if everyone's working remotely.' The creation of *Faith* was peppered with happy moments of chance, as we'll see, a paradoxically predictable side effect of having the freedom to let things flow.

And it wasn't just a matter of time. Chris Porter and George Michael found further space to stretch themselves in the lack of outside interference. 'One of the many beauties of working with George was absolutely zero A&R [Artists and Repertoire; the arm of the record label that keeps an eye on the artist, developing them, chivvying them along and reporting back to the bigwigs] influence. The label, Epic, wasn't on our backs at all. The only person we had any contact with on the business side was George's publisher, Dick Leahy.'

Dick Leahy, in partnership with Bryan Morrison, had been in Michael's corner since the early days of Wham!, providing invaluable encouragement and advice beyond the usual reach of your average music publisher. In the absence of a genuine manager at the very beginning, Leahy and Morrison were the closest thing. While they would weather the storm when Wham! extricated themselves from their notoriously mean contract with first label Innervision, they were actually brought into the picture by Innervision's main man Mark Dean, who had been mentored by Morrison and naturally turned to the pair when he wanted to get the Wham! bandwagon rolling. Dean, although smart, ambitious and well backed by CBS in the United States, was still relatively inexperienced, so needed the know-how that would turn a promising young band and songwriter's potential into big hits and top dollar. Leahy, as a music industry executive of a couple of decades' standing and co-founder of GTO

Records, had been around the block and knew the real deal when he saw it. 'They walked into the office and almost without hearing the songs you knew that they were going to make it,'[4] he told journalist Tony Parsons for *Bare*, the (auto-)biography Parsons and Michael wrote together in 1990. Of course, it helped that most of the songs on the demo tape Dean had given them were so strong. Leahy and Morrison heard 'Wham Rap!', 'Come On' and 'Club Tropicana' first of all, and while 'Come On' was a routine slice of pop-funk that would sound even less spectacular among the scintillating cohort of songs on side two of Wham!'s debut album *Fantastic* a year or so later, 'Wham Rap!' and 'Club Tropicana' demonstrated range, wit and melody. The publishers would get even more excited soon afterwards when they heard 'Careless Whisper' – according to Leahy, 'an outstanding, timeless piece of music'.[5] So, when the boys walked into the office in April 1982 and dazzled Leahy and Morrison with their image and presence, the publishers were already well aware it wasn't just style. And luckily for them, Michael and Andrew Ridgeley could spot the special ingredient in the older double act in front of them too.

As Wham! headed to a conclusion four years later, Michael also split ties with his and Ridgeley's management partnership, Simon Napier-Bell and Jazz Summers. They had come into the picture when Summers had approached Leahy and Morrison with a proposition to manage Wham! but the publishers had deemed him less than a major player. Summers had promptly persuaded former Yardbirds and Japan manager Napier-Bell to come on board with him as the heavyweight part of the package, and all of a sudden Leahy and Morrison were willing to talk. A whirlwind association that saw Wham! make it big all over the world and become, thanks to Napier-Bell's inveigling, the first Western pop act to play in China met a sticky end when the managers sold their company Nomis to Kunick Leisure, whose major shareholder Sol Kerzner, of Sun Hotels International, had intimate links to the Sun City entertainment complex in Apartheid-era South Africa. Michael was livid, finding out inadvertently when he and Wham!'s US tour booker Rob Kahane (later Michael's manager) saw newspaper headlines screaming, 'Wham! Sold to Sun City' and decided that was that. 'He went straight upstairs and fired them,' Kahane says now. Michael put out a press release officially serving notice of the dissolution of his agreement with Nomis (who retaliated with a release of their own, stating they were still working with Ridgeley, and therefore cascading the imminent Wham! split), and made it clear to Napier-Bell and Summers that he would only communicate through his lawyer Tony Russell – or Dick Leahy.

Through thick and thin, there was Leahy, a trusted voice and ear as Michael's solo career got underway. Back at Sarm West Studio 2 in Notting Hill, West London, he was an occasional visitor, but was careful not to stick an oar in. 'Dick would pop into the studio now and again,' continues Porter, 'and he was always just encouraging. He'd come in and listen and go, "Ah, this is going to be amazing." Otherwise, we never saw an A&R man from beginning to end, and I think that was part of the licence agreement George had with Sony at the time. We produced the records, they put them out.' Michael's dealings with the label would become more complex, the earlier Innervision wrangle a dry run for battles to come.

Sarm 2 was as happy a hunting ground for that creative spark as Puk. Its exposed position aside, the boho glamour of Notting Hill made for a beguiling location and, as Porter recalls, it attracted more than its fair share of music royalty. 'In the 1980s, it was heaving with pop genius. Every single room you'd walk past, there'd be a face. You'd have Boy George in one room, [Sheffield pop classicists] ABC in another with Trevor Horn – it was the place to be. The rooms had very good sound, great assistants and the standard of maintenance was high.'

Leahy did offer one morsel of – ostensibly significant – creative input when he suggested Michael try his hand at 1950s-style rock 'n' roll. The singer had the bare bones of 'Faith', the rhythm guitar introduction, and the publisher could hear a quick win, telling Michael how they would make a cut-and-shut instant hit back in the day, moving from guitar lick to bridge to outro, all in the blink of an eye. Apparently, Leahy dropped into the studio the next day to find the song complete and Michael saying, 'You mean like that?' 'Cheeky sod,'[6] Leahy told Parsons. But there's plenty of apocrypha surrounding 'Faith'. Another story surrounds the origins of the rhythm guitar Hugh Burns plays on the song, and it centres around Puk in Denmark, which rather suggests Leahy wasn't popping in at quite that point. Burns himself, in an interview with Andrew Brel for *Guitarist* magazine in 2002, is only drawn to say he's playing a 'nameless metal-bodied acoustic'[7] throughout the track – along with a Geffen custom Stratocaster for the solo – and he's right to be vague.

Chris Porter initially told *The Billboard Book of Number One Albums* that the guitar, 'this horrible aluminium-body guitar'[8] he recorded through a Neumann KM84 mic, belonged to original UK punks The Damned, who – according to one of the resident assistant engineers – had left it behind at Puk directly before Michael, Porter and the rest had moved in. Later, Porter recalled the aluminium guitar was blue and heart-shaped and was only played by Burns because his own guitars hadn't reached Denmark by the time work on the song began on 25 May 1987, and Michael – with the germ of an idea in his head – wanted to soldier on regardless. Session keyboard player Blue Weaver, an integral member of the Miami-era Bee Gees, was at Puk in 1986 recording The Damned's seventh album *Anything* and conjectured on Chris Porter's Facebook page that Damned guitarist Roman Jugg may have played the mystery instrument and left it there shortly before the *Faith* team arrived. The more prosaic truth seems to be that the guitar belonged to Puk Studio Manager Gunnar Balle, who had it shipped over from Sweden. Still, maybe Jugg did give it a strum? None of this precludes there being a molecule of old-school punk DNA in that 'Faith' riff. Assistant engineer Paul Gomersall, pulling in £400 a week, remembers it as a 'homemade thing. I was trying to get this sort of Bo Diddley sound and put this little auto-panner on it to make it more like a tremolo. That was on the SPX90 [Yamaha processor].' All this from a piece of junk. As Porter says, 'We knew it wasn't the best guitar in the world, but we could never better the sound for that part. Believe me, we tried. And that sound went on to tour the world! That guitar would be played out front with the other guitarist playing along with it. That very cheap, aluminium-bodied six-string.' The tale of the accidental guitar wasn't the only moment of kismet 'Faith' had up its sleeve.

As much as Michael wanted to put the past behind him and present a new face to the world, he couldn't help a nod to history. That church organ playing the melody to Wham!'s 'Freedom' on the intro to 'Faith' is a pang of nostalgia for a glorious period, a cheeky Easter egg for the fans and a full stop to an era all rolled into one. Surely forensically planned? Well, not quite. 'Oh, I was ribbing him,' says the man on the organ and other keys across the album, Chris Cameron. 'You see, I love Gustav Mahler [proto-modernist Bohemian composer of the late nineteenth and early twentieth centuries]. He's one of my favourite composers and I was telling George how melodic "Freedom" is and how, if you take away the Motown beat, the refined melody you're left with is actually very Mahlerian. It also has an "Englishness" about it I love,' he adds. 'But you could see it in his face: "Who is this bloody nutter?" So, I switched the Roland D-50 to "cathedral organ" mode and started playing. I slowed it right down and suddenly I could see a little lightbulb switch on over his head, and he put it down on tape.'

As he'd regularly discover, what Cameron considered to be a throwaway moment, or an unfinished contribution, would often be spun in his absence into something quite unforeseen. 'I didn't know it was going to be used for "Faith". It just came out of this conversation this mad keyboard player was having with him.' Cameron suspects that 'mad' chat may have struck a deeper chord, thinking, 'It may well have been the first time anybody had told him something he had done musically had that kind of worth. There I was comparing his work to Mahler, to Elgar too, and he's saying, "Oh no, I don't hear that," because he's just got that Motown thing in his head.' Cameron doesn't remember having any idea what the plan was for his cathedral organ skit until he heard the finished album, so there was an Easter egg for him as well.

The bare bones Dick Leahy had apparently heard in the first place were pretty much all that had been planned for 'Faith' – an interlude, an overture, before it got its own from Cameron – and Leahy isn't the only man to take credit for its expansion. 'George played me [what existed of] "Faith" at my house,' says Rob Kahane, by this stage Michael's manager (in partnership with Michael Lippman), 'and I said, "Wow, if you finished that song . . ." and he goes, "No, it's supposed to be finished. It's just an intro," and I said, "I'm telling you, that song's a fucking hit if you finish it." And like a lot of things I experienced with George, he then goes up to Vancouver, plays the record to the Sony people there, and calls me later saying, "You know, I think I'm gonna finish that 'Faith' song." It was like we'd never had the conversation.' A pivotal moment, as Kahane recognizes. 'So, he finished the song [at Sarm at the start of September 1987], and not only did it become the name of the album, but all the symbols for the album, everything happened because he finished it.' In Kahane's favour, Paul Gomersall corroborates at least some of his version of events. 'The manager walked in and went, "Oh man, this is a hit," and I was sitting there going, "Huh?" Because you know, compared to the other songs, it was the most stripped back and the most basic. It proved me wrong.'

Where Kahane was seduced by the immediacy of 'Faith', Gomersall was put off by its disregard for studio ingenuity. The businessman versus the craftsman.

Video director Andy Morahan – who'd worked with Michael on Wham! videos including 'Everything She Wants' and 'I'm Your Man', and would do the same for most of the ensuing *Faith* singles – made a virtue of the song's retro simplicity and set the new George Michael image in celluloid. 'He knew what he wanted to look like,' Morahan told the *Video Killed the Radio Star* mini-documentary series. 'His sister Mel and I drove down Melrose [Avenue, West Hollywood] the night before the shoot and bought the jacket and leathers and treasures – it was as simple as that.' Michael adds, 'I was so overly conscious of my image at that age, and so insecure, that I had actually developed a costume for real life – which was that – and I think the only thing that I added was the pearls. So, I knew there was a camp aspect to it and by then I'd had sex with men, so I was a little less clueless as to how to portray myself.'[9] 'I think George Michael has got far too smutty of late and I really don't like it one bit,'[10] gasped Lola Borg in her *Smash Hits* single review, while *NME*'s Sean O'Hagan conversely saw 'a rather tasteful Shakin' Stevens'.[11] Perhaps not the image he wanted to convey, but Michael knew what he was doing. That guitar he was flinging about served a purpose. 'I'm sure any guitar player is wetting themselves looking at the shapes I'm making with my hands,' he said, 'but Americans – if you stick a guitar on, you've got a bigger penis. It's as simple as that. Or you have one! In Wham! I didn't really have one.'[12]

Sex and the serious man

'The people behind Wham! are fucking them up something chronic,' Roland Orzabal of contemporaries Tears for Fears told UK music weekly *Melody Maker* in November 1983. 'They either have no self-respect or they're stupid or they're so worried that one day they're not gonna be a hit act.'[1] Perhaps that's why Andrew Ridgeley – with an enjoyably long memory – voted Orzabal for Worst Male Singer, Worst Female Singer, Worst Dressed Person, Worst Haircut and Worst Thing in the World (oh, and Worst Prat? 'Curt Smith for being linked with Roland Orzabal'[2]) in the 1985 *Smash Hits* Readers' Poll. Anyway, Orzabal was ranting about a centrespread in right-leaning UK tabloid the *Daily Express*, somewhere no pop star of integrity should be, but he pinpointed the essential Wham! condition all the same. The need to please, to hang onto an audience. *Faith* was about losing those fans, in the nicest possible way – not that it quite had the desired effect. 'I expected to be dealing with a completely different audience on this tour,' George Michael admitted to *Q* magazine in 1988 following the dazzlingly successful *Faith* shows. 'I expected a lot less screaming and I didn't really get what I wanted.'[3] Still, it wasn't for lack of a plan, and Michael's plan was as hot as his Wham!-era pants.

There are few better ways to say, 'Hey, I'm not really the cheesy guy in gym shorts and detergent-white T-shirts' than getting on up like a sex machine. Coming up to a year after torpedoing Wham! and all that teenage innocence at *The Final* farewell gig, Michael released 'I Want Your Sex', an affirmation of his new, muskier image and lyrical proof that there was more than just a shuttlecock rammed down those shorts. Accompanied by a video – again directed by Andy Morahan – featuring then-girlfriend Kathy Jeung in her smalls at the very most, and real and stunt Georges exhibiting varying amounts of flesh, this was a package designed to make more mature consumers – and censors – sit up and take notice.

One was potentially scotched by the other, though, as the gatekeepers got to work, blocking the single's route to sympathetic ears. British decency campaigner Mary Whitehouse – think Tipper Gore without the stickers – took a surprisingly restrained position, arguing that 'the tone of the lyrics is out of keeping with sexual trends activated because of AIDS,'[4] where you'd usually expect her to take exception to the lyrics, the title and the suggestive sleeve (bodies vividly writhing under silk sheets even in a photo still) for their mere existence. The BBC was more enthusiastic with the censorship hammer, pushing any Radio 1 airplay to after the 9.00 p.m. 'watershed' (the safe hour when susceptible children were sure to be in bed, possibly tucked under the covers listening to scandalous songs on the radio through concealed headphones) and, in a spectacular display of prurience, refusing to even mention the song's title on the

Top of the Pops chart rundown at prime time every Thursday evening. 'I don't think anybody's heard it, have they?' asked Michael in his contemporary interview with Jonathan Ross. 'I literally have not heard it on the radio.'[5] Millions of people watched George Michael climb to the upper reaches of the hit parade with an entirely anonymous record. 'I'm very proud of the record,' Michael insisted, 'but the ban was to be fully expected.'[6]

It was a similar story in the United States, where *American Top 40* mainstay Casey Kasem also couldn't bear to let 'I Want Your Sex' pass his lips. To the untrained eye, George Michael was flying up the charts on both sides of the Atlantic on the strength of his name alone. Well, he wouldn't be unique there, but adherents to the name would be old fans, those who had refused to be jettisoned alongside Andrew Ridgeley, those who had hung on as Michael was blown away by Aretha Franklin's peerless pipes on 'I Knew You Were Waiting (For Me)'. The old faithful sent 'I Want Your Sex' to number three in the UK and number two in the United States, no mean feat on either side. But were there new buyers in the mix? Not if the casual listener couldn't get anywhere near it. Shooting for a sexy new image, Michael blew his load in his own foot.

Those happy to buy before they tried would have found an artist raunching up not just his lyrical content but also his sound. Michael had been edging down the auteur route for some time, from the earliest days of Wham!, gradually taking control of the compositional and recording process. It hadn't taken long to realize Ridgeley, while a useful foil for the trials and flashbulbs of pop stardom, hardly possessed the skills to pen sure-fire hits, so Michael had swiftly taken sole ownership of songwriting duties, to no discernible protest. He was barely less speedy taking his place in the producer's chair, getting to move a few faders on Wham!'s 1983 debut album *Fantastic*, then doing the full job on the 1984 follow-up *Make It Big*. What he hadn't done was go full writer/singer/producer/performer, the ultimate mark of the pop genius he so desperately wanted to appear to be if he was going to be taken as seriously as he hoped, but *Faith* gave him the opportunity. 'I don't have any guilt that I can now call the shots in my career,'[7] he told *Record Mirror*'s Eleanor Levy on the release of 'I Want Your Sex'. The reams of performer credits had been whittled down from the cast of thousands on *Fantastic* to the manageable team of session players on *Make It Big* and then a close-knit squad (horn section aside) on *Faith*. Here and there though, and most notably on 'I Want Your Sex (Part I)', Michael went it alone.

So far, so Prince. So very Prince, if we're picking up the hints. 'Part I' of the cannily named 'Monogamy Mix', and the radio edit if anyone got to hear it, is sparse and funky, an ostensible cousin to 'Sign "☮" the Times' – just as stark, a little more propulsion. Michael's effort might not have been directly influenced by it, coming so hot on its heels just four months later, but it bears the Prince hallmarks of sinuous economy and pared-down slinkiness, and most importantly – in the pursuit of that elusive, adult credibility – it carries the legend 'All instruments: George Michael'. In 2022, every man jack with a laptop or an effects box is a self-producing multi-instrumentalist with all-encompassing creative control, but in 1987 this was god-tier artistry, the realm of Prince and Michael's hero Stevie Wonder, legends who had earned the right. Credibility, opportunity, dues paid – new territory for the former singer of a bubblegum pop band.

'He gets so little credit as an instrumentalist and as a producer,' reckons Paul Gambaccini. 'He made that album by himself in the same way Stevie made his 1970s albums and Prince all his records – and that really puts you into a different state of mind. Like Paul McCartney too, playing piano, guitar, drums. If you're in that extremely rarefied club, you're necessarily competing.' Andy Duncan, percussionist on 'Hand to Mouth' further into the album, agrees. 'Some people say George was a control freak, but that tends to be a pejorative term, and no one would say that about Stevie Wonder. George was similar in the way he had a phenomenal ability to conceptualize a piece of music and keep it in his head. He didn't get involved in the technicalities of Synthi code and synchronization and MIDI offsets and all that. He couldn't care less. What he could do was compare what somebody else might be offering to what he had in his head. And a lot of the time, he wanted to try and do it himself just because he could.' 'George never worried about mic selection or technicalities of that sort – that was my area,' confirms Chris Porter. 'In fact, he never really learned to play an instrument, to be truthful. He played some great stuff, of course, but his playing was very "three fingers". "Last Christmas" is a great example of that – it's the "Chopsticks" of pop.'

To play Prince at his own game, however, you really have to go the distance. Prowl, purr and get priapic. Later in their careers, Michael and Prince would find they had more in common as they scrapped for artistic control against their respective record labels, even if Prince went for it with typical ostentation – 'slave' etched on the cheek and all that – while

Michael kept it sober, but they weren't likely bedfellows in 1987. To work his way into that headspace, Michael had to get lascivious – natural, chemical and assertive; counterintuitive moods for the Michael we had known up to this point, but necessary if he was to achieve the dual target of upgrading his audience and competing on level terms with the best in the game. While you don't have to be a sex god to achieve a number one single, you might want to consider acting like one if you want to be the biggest pop star on the planet.

The Prince impression is a qualified success. 'I Want Your Sex' is a beautifully poised chug through machine-tooled grooves and saucy suggestions that, as a single, deserved much more than its restricted audience. It betrays its apprentice loverman though. For all the sensual build-up, the finale of 'Part I' is Michael at his most gauche. Canvassing definitions of filth is surely intended as a leer, a liberated willingness to transgress, but it comes off like a suitor who hasn't found the right words, has half-heard that this is the kind of thing the ladies – and 'I Want Your Sex' is explicitly directed at a girl – want to be asked if you're getting anywhere near your goal. By the last few seconds, he's not even as delicate as that, his questions more insistent than curious. It's not subtle. No one ever accused Prince of subtlety either. Gratifyingly, the references were picked up by the critics, with Barry McIlheney of *Smash Hits* noting the 'grunting and funk rhythms so favoured by the King Perv',[8] *NME*'s Michele Kirsch claiming it 'out-Princes Prince'[9] and *Record Mirror*'s Lesley O'Toole disparaging 'a misguided attempt at swiping Prince's immovable "king of tack" tag'.[10] But, of course, George Michael can never go full Rogers Nelson, not when his natural instincts poke through. The triumphal section of the brass-fuelled 'I Want Your Sex (Part II)', the 'Rhythm 2: Brass in Love' mix, is way too obviously melodic, quashing the funk of 'Part I' and the horny soul of the transition to go somewhere nakedly euphoric. Prince wouldn't waver in his pursuit of the groove.

By this point, Michael has ceded ground, not just to the horn players but also to seasoned session guitarist Robert Ahwai and bassist Deon Estus, the latter having been such an integral member of Wham!'s backing band that he'd taken prominent roles in the videos of a superficially two-man act. Not everything – nor everyone – had been left behind for the new beginning. Estus – who sadly died in October 2021 – had seen the smile, now he saw the smoulder.

Of course, in a parallel universe, it could have been another old sparring partner – David Austin – panting for monogamy and wriggling about under the silk sheets in the video instead. Alongside 'Look at Your Hands' (more on that later), when sessions began at Sarm West Studio 2 in August 1986, 'I Want Your Sex' had been earmarked as one of a couple of potential catalysts for Austin's somewhat stalled solo career, but Austin was more likely to be swinging a guitar around than anything else and the fit just wasn't there. 'When we got to Puk [the following February],' reveals assistant engineer Paul Gomersall, 'George just said, "I've got this song . . . " as if nothing had happened.' Speaking about the song in 1990, Michael said, 'I'd written this song for someone else six months before and people said, "Why don't you do it?" But I thought I couldn't do it; it was too far away from what I normally write. And then I thought, "Why not?" I knew it wasn't a huge risk and it wasn't going to finish me, but it did jar my track record in England.'[11] The scandal of a George Michael song that didn't make it to number one. Maybe the fans weren't ready for its horny squeaks and squirts.

Incredibly, all that terribly (in)appropriate gurgling and grinding isn't the product of judicious sound effects; it's just fate stepping in again. Settling in at Puk, the singer and the ever-present engineer Porter wired up the equipment – a Roland Juno-60, LinnDrum and Yamaha DX7, Neumann and Shure mics – and let the magic take care of itself. 'We plugged up this drum machine and for some reason it started playing all these strange noises – random bursts of percussion and squelches,' says Porter. Instead of inventing acid house a few months early or just resetting the machines to something more conventional, they chose to follow the funk. 'We just went, "That's kind of cool, isn't it?" and then started to try and integrate it into a rhythm track.' Speaking to *Sound On Sound* magazine in 2013, Porter credits Michael with recognizing the potential of the odd bleeps and glitches before the engineer pulled the plug again: 'I said, "It's a bit weird," and he said, "Yeah, but if we just take a bit out of here and a bit out of there we might be able to use it."'[12] Always mindful of Michael's nose (and ear) for a winning concept, Porter leapt right in.

While not exactly a regular event, catching lightning in a bottle was at least a possibility in the recording studios of the mid- to late 1980s, if only because the technology wasn't quite on point, or lacked the experts to control it. 'In those days, when the tech was at a fairly early stage and we were running things off Synthi or MIDI, it was all very unfamiliar,' says Porter. 'There was a lot of new machinery coming out and trying to set it all up and get each component to talk to each other often resulted in strange occurrences. And of course, at that time, there were so many external elements to the recording process – in fact, virtually everything was external, whereas now, with computer recording, everything's internal so accidents are less likely to happen. You actually have to go looking for your accidents in the digital domain.'

With the serendipity in the bag, the pair set about constructing the rest of the song, and – eventually – the other two sections that made up the complete 'Monogamy Mix' that would appear on the 12-inch single and, in pieces, across the extended *Faith* album. The first part adopted the typical Michael practice of laying it down four bars at a time, the singer controlling all of those unpredictable machines himself. There was also a Greengate DS:3 sampler in the mix (a new toy used first here and then elsewhere on the album), although Porter would mainly trigger samples using the AMS delay, the Advanced Music Systems daddy of digital delay. This spirit of technical discovery is a crucial constituent of the project. 'That's largely what *Faith* is about,' reckons Porter. 'It's about George starting to explore what he could do on his own. As the recording process unfolded over the course of a year and a bit, we started off with a full bunch of musicians in the studio and gradually the players that are all in the studio at the same time begin to reduce, and then it's George and a couple of people in the room and sometimes just George and me. He was really excited about all the things he could do.'

He was equally excited about all the things he could exclude. 'There was a certain kind of musicianship he tended not to like,' Porter continues. 'What would you call it? Virtuosity? Trademarks, perhaps. As a session musician, if you played a favourite lick, he'd spot it straight away and he'd just say, irritably, "Could you stop doing that?"' It casts new light on the young Michael's irritation with all those sax players at Muscle Shoals who couldn't reproduce the solo in his head, but Porter thinks 'part of it was, he was always aware that he had to keep his vocal as the main instrument and the best way to achieve that was to sweep all other musical clutter out of the way'. Decades on, Porter recognizes afresh how those vocals take centre stage. 'What comes across to me now is the vocal textures, the layering of vocals and the different voices he uses. All sorts of fun experiments.' It's always clear how focused Michael was on what he wanted, but it wasn't about expertise, it was about feel.

At the extreme end of the exclusion scale, sometimes musicians had to be let go altogether, and that wasn't George's job. 'When we were in the States,' says Porter, 'we worked with one or two heavyweight session players, one of which we spent all day wiring up then working with before George took me aside and said, "I don't like what he's doing – do you think we could get rid of him?" So, I had to try to find the nicest way to sack people. It wasn't a matter of quality – usually they were amazing – it was just they had their "thing" and George had his.'

To balance it out, Porter also had the responsibility of hiring people for the job, people who got to stick around and who'd often been around for some time already. There's a sense on *Faith* of getting the old band back together, musicians like

Robert Ahwai, Hugh Burns and Deon Estus, who'd played with Wham! and had also contributed to Michael's earlier solo excursions. 'As you can imagine,' Porter says, 'we had opportunities to work with all sorts of fantastic people, but George tended to like people he knew and trusted, even if sometimes they had limitations. It was more that he could communicate with them easily and they would do what he wanted.'

'Rhythm 1: Lust' of 'I Want Your Sex' was all about Michael acting alone. 'Rhythm 2: Brass in Love' and 'Rhythm 3: A Last Request' were collective affairs with those collaborators he could trust, brought together at Puk Studios. 'The environment was completely different,' says keyboard player Chris Cameron. 'I remember the snow and a huge studio with a lovely vibe, out in the countryside.' Cameron was a new addition to the George Michael circle, but he was hooking up with an old band too. 'It was a good team there – we had a laugh, because we all knew each other. [Trumpet player] Steve Sidwell and all the brass players had been with me in the National Youth Jazz Orchestra, so we all got along famously. It was great to see Rick Taylor – the trombone player – again, as well as Paul Spong.'

Familiar support on the two new tracks came from Estus and Ahwai, on bass and guitar respectively, and another keyboard player, Danny Schogger (who had made his Wham! debut late in the game on the valedictory 'The Edge of Heaven' EP), adding some lovely clavinet. The album feels like it's taking flight, but Michael was making it up as he went along, writing in the studio as each line suggested itself from the chord sequences. At the desk, Porter was taking all the disparate elements and using the patented Porter/Michael method of constructing tracks. They'd do it in pieces and glue it all together. 'The desk at Puk had 28 channels on either side, so I had the original multitrack on one side and what would be the new version on the other side,' Porter told *Sound on Sound*. 'I was bouncing from the master over to the slave for the crossover point as the musicians went into this new section, and George would tell them, "Play something like this," they'd rehearse the part and we'd drop it in. If it didn't work, we'd drop it in again.'[13] That went on for several hours, giving the horn players nice, chapped lips – but they enjoyed themselves out there. Trumpet player Steve Sidwell, who had recorded with Wham! in the early years and would go on to enjoy a fruitful creative relationship with Michael, right up to taking the musical director role on his *Symphonica* tour twenty-five years later, remembers honing his sporting skills. 'We [the horn section] went out to Denmark for four or five days and we did wait around a bit. We improved our table tennis. Hanging around was always part of the process. We'd be booked for a day and they'd say, "OK, chill out for a few hours; we need to do something else." I don't remember thinking we were wasting our time. There was always something creative going on.' However irregularly they were called upon, the horn section always swung, bringing a suit-and-spats panache to the song's later phases.

Back in the Wham! days, Sidwell recalls wilder times, but Michael wasn't quite one of the lads. 'Before we realized he wasn't partying in the same way we were – hanging out and chasing women all over the place – he was in his room with his Walkman on. You'd say, "What did you do last night?" and he'd say he just went to bed listening to this or that. I was thinking, "You're one of the biggest superstars on the planet, we're all in our 20s, we're going around America and all these people like us, and you're going to bed listening to music." But that was his passion.'

As Sidwell admits, there was plenty he hadn't realized. Michael had half come out to his best friends before Wham! had really hit pay dirt, but in an interview with *Gay Times* in 2007, he revealed he'd been cruising since he was a teen in Radlett and Bushey on the northwest outskirts of London. Telling Ridgeley and Holliman he was bisexual was a sign of losing his nerve, of not wanting to face the consequences – the commercial consequences even – of saying he was gay. 'Within two years we were the biggest pop band in America and, it's like, what the fuck are you going to do?' he said to *Gay Times*. 'You have the option of hiding, and you have some attraction to women at least – what else are you going to do at that age? When you're more successful than you ever dreamed you were going to be?'[14] Throughout the first fifteen years of his career, Michael was habitually asked if he was gay, and he would neither confirm nor deny, insisting that the need to know said more about his interlocutors than him. Occasionally though, there'd be a telling remark. Pursued for an answer by *NME*'s Danny Kelly in 1985, he said, 'Obviously if I said [I'm gay] that'd be completely different. But the fact remains that it only takes someone to say it to a paper and they'll print it. I can sue them but they'll still have ruined my career.'[15] The belief – probably well founded in the 1980s – that it would destroy all he'd built is at least as persuasive a reason why Michael didn't come out as the later suggestion that he was sparing his parents.

Naturally, it puts a different spin on Michael's cavorting with Kathy Jeung in the 'I Want Your Sex' video and campaign, and indeed on their relationship. His story shifted over the years. The obfuscation made for a confusing message around the single's release. Chris Heath of *Smash Hits* tried to get to the truth by increments, asking about the record sleeve's dedication to 'my hopeless conquest'. 'Well actually the song was written about two relationships mixed up,' answered Michael. 'The "hopeless conquest" one doesn't really make sense anymore and I tried to get that quote removed but it was too late. It doesn't fit with the other sleevenote about my actual current long-term relationship, saying that I believe in the idea of lust within a loving relationship.'[16] Ah yes, 'lust within a loving relationship'. Daubing 'explore monogamy' in lipstick on Jeung's naked back in the video was supposed to head off the Mary Whitehouses and Tipper Gores and deflect AIDS-related criticism – and certainly Michael was sensitive to that. 'I still believe in monogamy as an ideal,'[17] he insisted to *The Advocate* in 1999, but he'd really wanted to make a good old bump'n'grind record. 'I didn't have the courage of my convictions, did I?' he told *Gay Times*. Carrying on, he disclosed he 'genuinely had written the song about a man I couldn't get to fuck and sleep with me. Even though I knew he was fucking crazy about me. He was the guy I was in love with when I was with Kathy, who was definitely in love with me at that time ... "I Want Your Sex" was directly about being tired of waiting for this French guy – so I was writing about all that confusion.'[18]

Despite pushing the song's assumed social conscience by stressing its promotion of monogamy 'in a [US] national radio special and during an unusual introduction to his video, done for MTV'[19] – as contemporary press noted – not everyone was figuratively buying it. 'Obviously I wasn't pretending there wouldn't be any controversy,' he told UK newspaper *The Guardian*. 'I was looking forward to the controversy. I just wouldn't have believed it would be so incredibly negative and thoughtless.'[20] If he wanted to land his social politics, Michael would need to be more sincere.

Politics (the pop remix)

At the start of 1987, *Melody Maker*'s news section announced the imminent release of 'I Knew You Were Waiting (For Me)', George Michael's soon-to-be chart-topping duet with Aretha Franklin, and snuck in a teaser for what was coming down the line. Easter promised Michael's first solo single proper after the Wham! split and it sounded like an AA-side. 'The two tracks are called "Betcha Don't Like It", "a love song about a young mother married to a drunk," and "I Want Your Sex", "a saucy number along the lines of Prince's Kiss,"'[1] went the titbit, and while we all know which won out in the end, the fate of both songs could have been entirely different.

Like 'I Want Your Sex', 'Betcha Don't Like It' – or 'Look at Your Hands', to give it its final title on *Faith* – was another potential career boost intended for Michael's pal David Austin. A chunk of barrelhouse boogie, swinging its rather trad rock'n'roll hips, it's something of an outlier on *Faith*, so there's sense in its original destination. Ostensibly, it's a raucous, good-time tune that shares the brashness of Austin's 1984 debut solo single 'Turn to Gold', if not its lyrical content, and packs the musical punch of any good breakthrough hit. But again like 'Turn to Gold' (a near-miss at number 68 on the UK singles chart) and the parallel-world 'I Want Your Sex', it wasn't to be. Austin had been around from the start – Michael's best mate since primary school – and had stayed on the scene even as they went on to separate high schools. He was as crucial a part of his friend's dawning musical career as Andrew Ridgeley had been. As teens, Michael and Austin (or David Mortimer as he was then) would bunk off school and dash to London to play for coins as buskers on the London Underground, and later on Austin would join Michael and Ridgeley in The Executive, the ska band whose implosion set Wham! in motion. At that stage, Austin wasn't prepared to throw his lot in with the pair. Instead, after the demise of The Executive, he sloped off on a jaunt to East Asia, telling Michael 'if his songs were any good they would have been signed up already'.[2]

He changed his tune a few months down the line when the whirlwind of the Innervision signing and then a fortuitous late drop-out saw them gifted a spot on the 4 November 1982 edition of *Top of the Pops* with second single 'Young Guns (Go For It)', despite it breaking one of the show's stone-tablet rules by skulking just outside the Top 40 at number 42. Find the surviving clip from a couple of weeks later and you'll see Austin frugging away on a guitar, jeans rolled up away from his espadrilles just like Yog (Michael's persistent childhood nickname) and Andy, pulling off the kind of mime Ridgeley would make his own. This big-gang Wham! of Michael, Ridgeley, Austin, backing singers/dancers Dee C Lee and Shirlie Holliman, Deon Estus on bass and Andrew's brother Paul Ridgeley on drums was, in varying forms, a fixture of the early TV appearances. But Austin soon lost his guitar, performing backing vocals on *Top of the Pops* for the successful January 1983 rerelease of debut single 'Wham Rap! (Enjoy What You Do)' and then disappearing altogether by the time 'Bad Boys' narrowly missed the UK chart zenith in May. He had his reasons. Apart from there being no room in the spotlight for anyone but Michael and Ridgeley (and Lee and Holliman as far as TV appearances and videos went), Austin – or Mortimer as he was still known – had irons in the fire. In September, *Melody Maker* reports, 'Former Wham! guitarist Dave Mortimer is close to a record deal for his group Grapes (previously Fantastic),[3] a name doubtless dropped around the time Wham! were giving it to their debut album – or perhaps it was nabbed? As for Mortimer's band's current name, *Smash Hits* probably heard right when they say it's 'Great'[4] rather than Grapes. Mortimer is said to be 'co-writing with Wham!'s George Michael. A single, "Golden Soul" is due out shortly, featuring Mortimer on vocals and not guitar.'[5] An important distinction. Equally intriguingly, we learn that Mortimer has 'written and produced a record for Boney M's Lisa Paradise. "Real Guys (Never Get Lonely)" is coming out before Christmas.'[6] And that's the last we hear from either until Austin rears up on British kids' TV show *Cheggers Plays Pop* on 5 June 1984, performing his new single 'Turn to Gold', introduced by his old mucker George.

A couple of years on, it was time to have another crack at that elusive pop stardom. 'Look at Your Hands' was worked up at Sarm West in September 1986, at that instant very much a David Austin song, but with Michael, inevitably, heavily involved. David Fricke was in the room for *Rolling Stone*, noting that 'the song appears to be just a few hours away from completion, lacking only a couple of verses, overdubs and a tighter lead vocal',[7] and that even though Michael was laying down the vocal part, it would simply be a guide for Austin's final version. Austin himself was there too, banging out the riff alongside co-guitarist JJ Belle, while elsewhere on the song was keyboard player Danny Schogger – more from him later. As it goes, Fricke's assessment was optimistic, and 'Look at Your Hands' was more months than hours away from its final form. 'We worked on that track on and off for a year before the lyric was actually finished and it was actually decided it would go on the album,' remembers engineer Chris Porter. As for how it switched from being an Austin song to a Michael song: 'Painfully!' admits Porter. 'It was a protracted process. The song was written by David and George together, and the premise of the track was that it was very Stonesy, with very rocky riffs, a complete departure, really. I don't think you'll find another George Michael track anything like it.' To put his own stamp on it, Michael looked to Porter for some customary tricks. 'I don't know quite how George thought it satisfactorily became his – I think by the addition of a lot of reverb!' Paul Gomersall adds that it's probably 'lucky' that Michael didn't leave 'Look at Your Hands' with his friend, 'because David probably made 100 times more than he would have done if he'd recorded it himself. Apparently, he got very upset George decided to do it by himself. I wouldn't have.'

There's a certain sketchiness to memories around 'Look at Your Hands', possibly a side effect of circumstance – a mixture of guilt, lack of familiarity with the style, a bit of moonlighting. Austin, although credited as co-writer, is billed as Lord Monty in the personnel list, hiding him from the searchlights of the executives at EMI, where he was signed at the time. Schogger, the keyboard player who contributed to 'I Want Your Sex' later on, has no recollection of the recording at all. He remembers the guitarist JJ Belle ('lovely guy') and has fond things to say about playing alongside Michael in general ('really talented and very enjoyable to work with'), but of Schogger's own thrilling, freewheeling solo on 'Look at Your Hands'? Not a glimmer. That's the price of a successful session career. You're in, you do your thing, you're out. But perhaps it also says a little about 'Look at Your Hands' overall. It belonged to someone else. Something wasn't quite there. *Melody Maker*'s Steve Sutherland certainly felt it belonged to someone else – 'It's The Specials' 'Too Much Too Young' rewritten actually'[8] – but Austin had a real grip on it for a while.

Paul Gambaccini feels the whole idea was doomed to fail. 'He tried to make David a star', he says, 'but no matter how badly you would like to share some of your success with your friends, you can't. The public won't respond.' However, you can ensure your buddy keeps his co-writing credit and help his pension fund along like that. Loyalty's a two-way street, of course; Austin eventually parked his own dreams and stepped back into the Michael machine, still seeking out commercial opportunities and running the music side of the George Michael Estate to this day.

The billowy rhythm 'n' blues setting wasn't the only uncharacteristic slant to 'Look at Your Hands'; it also delivered a bite in its lyric, a hint of vérité to separate it from pop platitudes. That quote in *Melody Maker* – 'a love song about a young mother married to a drunk' – is a functional but flippant summary of a song that tackles domestic abuse from the viewpoint of the bitter white knight who wants to take the mother away from it all. Once he was beyond the teen petulance of 'Bad Boys', Michael had made wry observations about slightly more grown-up relationship drama with 'Everything She Wants' or even 'Credit Card Baby', but hadn't got right down in the grime. Here was an opportunity to bring a sociological issue to bear, drawing from headlines and some detached personal experience, although he deliberately avoids telling the story from the very centre of the maelstrom. 'The thing was David's backing track was quite sexy so I felt I had to write the song from the point of view of someone outside the situation,'[9] he told *No. 1* magazine. It's a tool that allows for ambiguity. The shock of hearing that the husband is hitting his wife is hardly leavened by our narrator effectively sneering at what she's left with. Sure, he's been rebuffed for this violent drunk, but it's a funny kind of help on offer. Even Michael seems to draw odd conclusions, telling *No. 1*, 'He's saying to this woman, "come away with me," even though she's got these two kids. It's like one of those 50s movies where a kid gets involved with a sleazy older woman.'[10] There's a jarring sense of misogyny to the song and the conversation around it, an uncomfortable fit in the Michael catalogue.

In the news bulletin section of *Faith*, 'Look at Your Hands' is joined by 'Hand to Mouth' where – before swinging back to the UK to peer through a bedroom window – the camera swoops around the flashpoints of the United States. In 1987, everyone in the British Isles was making their great observational record about Uncle Sam, capturing America's vast geographical and political sweep in a pithy swish of synecdoche. The Proclaimers were writing it in a letter, Deacon Blue surveyed its post-bomb fallout through the features of a former scientist's face in 'He Looks Like Spencer Tracy Now', and U2, naturally, prepared themselves to encapsulate its very soul (and capture its very market). Eight months ahead of *Faith*, U2's *The Joshua Tree* had delivered its own state of another nation address, taking a particularly stinging look at America's foreign policy on 'Bullet the Blue Sky', a leaden but brutally effective protest song kicking off at the devastation wrought by US military intervention in Central America. As it drags to a resigned finish, U2 vocalist Bono sees the displaced locals flee towards America's embrace, seeking a new home in the country that ruined the old one. He stands in ironic judgement, a reserve he'd jettison eighteen months later with double-album hagiography *Rattle and Hum*.

Whether by design, mischief or just accident, Michael's 'Hand to Mouth' finds its protagonist running into those arms as well. There's a suggestion it's actually an escape from one set of jaws to another, because the American Dream's an illusion and any cycle of violence, poverty or depravity is doomed to continue whatever the environment. Indeed, it'll be mirrored on either side of the Atlantic. Michael's overarching theme is split into several vignettes – the hopeless young gunman on a killing spree, the child of a prostitute left on a doorstep, the destitute fending for themselves as bright young things are elevated – and while he still believes in an answer early in the song, by the end he's desperately trying to convince himself his prayers will be heard one day. He'll make a habit of praying for time. The brief story of disaffected, gun-toting Jimmy was inspired by the Los Angeles freeway shootings of the summer of 1987, where more than sixty seemingly random incidents over the course of three months saw the deaths of at least five people. Michael, in Los Angeles at the time, felt the wave of paranoia engulf the city and was moved to write a song with the winningly direct title 'Gun Control', getting two verses down before further nightmarish circumstance stayed his hand. 'The week after I came back Hungerford happened,' he told *No.1*, referring to one of Britain's worst mass shootings when, on 19 August 1987, Michael Ryan tore his hometown of Hungerford, Berkshire asunder, shooting sixteen people dead including his own mother before killing himself. 'Can you imagine what would have happened if I'd come out with that song?'[11] Michael added. Some controversy isn't worth courting.

His solution was to broaden the reach of the lyric. As he pools the social injustices on each side of the pond, 'Hand to Mouth' becomes an indictment of both Margaret Thatcher and Ronald Reagan, of the drawbridge being pulled up. Thatcher is the protagonist running to America, where she finds reward but only for herself. 'The lyric is pretty good for somebody of that age,' Michael confided to Mark Goodier in the liner notes to the *Faith: Legacy Edition* rerelease. 'It's very anti-Thatcher. It's all about Thatcher and Reagan really but I don't think I'd express it that much better if I did it today.' He accepted it could only ever have been a detour. 'I was, ultimately, very tempted to be an activist in some form, but I knew that no one would really listen very hard to that.'[12] It was a question of audience expectation. Everyone had their own idea of what a George Michael record should sound like and what it should address. Some would give him leeway, others preferred him to stay in his pop box and shut up. And he'd been knocked back inside it before.

There was nothing apolitical about Wham! in the early days, however shallow 'Club Tropicana' or 'Bad Boys' might have felt. 'Young Guns (Go For It)' was sharp teen satire, 'Wham Rap! (Enjoy What You Do)' made sardonic hay with dole-queue nihilism. While one early interview found them insisting they were 'definitely aiming for an escapist market,'[13] and their first *NME* feature had Michael equivocating, 'What we are saying in ['Wham! Rap'] is that unemployment is there ... you might as well have a laugh about it,'[14] another teased Michael into saying, 'I'm sorely tempted to write something expressing disapproval with the obvious wrongs that are going on in this country.'[15] Not quite incendiary stuff, but a sign at least of where his vote was going.

With 1984 came freedom from the suffocating strictures of the Innervision deal, big CBS bucks on the table and the huge hits to justify them. Now Michael and Ridgeley could turn their attention to the rest of the world. The first obvious emblem of political engagement was a prominent slot at the benefit gig to mark the grand finale of Five Nights for the Miners at the Greater London Council's (GLC) Royal Festival Hall in London on 7 September 1984. The series of gigs had been arranged to support the National Union of Mineworkers (NUM) in their industrial action to prevent the UK government from shutting down at least 20 – by later accounts up to 75 – of the existing 173 collieries (coal mines) across the country, and were spearheaded by the more famously left-wing likes of Paul Weller and New Order. Wham!'s scheduled appearance was a surprise, albeit a welcome one for the coffers, and a sitting duck for the pure-rock, anti-pop critics in the audience and the media. The band didn't exactly help themselves. From the start, according to *NME*'s Nick Kent, 'something was clearly wrong – the sound emitted was not booming from the amps because no one hunched over his instrument was plugged in.'[16] Evidently Wham! were miming, just as their ideological enemies hoped, and a breakdown during 'Wake Me Up Before You Go-Go' made it clear. While Kent managed a backhanded compliment, seeing Wham!'s very presence as a portent they had 'something to say beyond the doltish clichés emblazoned across their designer T-shirts and the feckless bourgeois bop of their tacky pop songs',[17] *Melody Maker*'s Adam Sweeting was scathing, claiming their performance 'demonstrated no taste and less intelligence'.[18] Both observed that Michael was defiant, insisting that worrying about whether Wham! were really playing their instruments was missing the point of the evening. But if he was hoping to win new hearts and minds, it was an own goal.

The fallout continued throughout the rest of the year. *Melody Maker*'s Colin Irwin followed up the story in November, poking the beast with questions about Wham!'s motives. While Michael deftly danced around the politics of the miners' strike itself, he sounded sincere when he said it was concern for the families' welfare that drove them. Still, Irwin got his scoop. On being asked if he saw an end to the miners' dispute, Michael was 'very sceptical actually. We met Arthur Scargill [then president of the NUM] after and I think he is a wanker. . . . I got the impression he was a bit of a megalomaniac.'[19] His conclusion was, with Scargill on their side and Thatcher against them, the miners were stuck between the proverbial rock and hard place, and his comments had fun results. Just over a week after their publication, on 25 November, Michael found himself at Sarm West for the recording of Band Aid's 'Do They Know It's Christmas?' – another conspicuously altruistic act – in the same room as Paul Weller, former Jam frontman, now leader of The Style Council, a fellow performer at the Royal Festival Hall, staunch supporter of Scargill and, according to Michael, 'the only person there who didn't seem to succumb to the charitable nature of the day'. Taking umbrage at the quotes about Scargill, Weller 'decided to attack [Michael] in front of everybody', that 'everybody' being a who's who of British pop's glamorous mid-1980s heyday. Michael dismissed him in familiar terms: ' "Don't be a wanker all your life," I said. "Have a day off." '[20] The Miners' Benefit had been a frustrating experience for Wham! who 'were there to do people some good, and all we got were insults. . . . The fact that we were miming is irrelevant. Our band can play better than The Style Council's.'[21]

There had been another telling line in Irwin's *Melody Maker* interview, but it would take three decades for it to reveal its full meaning. 'When we do things for charity,' Michael declared, 'we don't go around screaming about it.'[22] Most of Michael's gifts to society would fly under the radar, only surfacing after his death when newspaper articles began listing examples of his generosity, from consistent support for children's charity Childline (which received royalties from his 1996 UK number one and US top 10 single 'Jesus to a Child') and AIDS charity the Terrence Higgins Trust to small acts of kindness towards people whose stories had touched him – paying for IVF treatment for a contestant on TV game show *Deal or No Deal*; wiping a student nurse's debt after hearing her woes – to a dedicated 'concert free of charge for nurses as a thank you for the care they had given his mother'.[23] For the few years after Band Aid, however, as pop found its conscience and slapped it on badges, T-shirts and several collective number one singles, Michael – and often Ridgeley too – were prominent participants in a succession of statement events. Superficial compassion soon began to pall. Speaking to *Life* magazine in the aftermath of the Nelson Mandela 70th Birthday Tribute concert held at Wembley Stadium on 11 June 1988, where he had performed a series of covers, Michael reckoned 'charity is a fashion that has now passed. This time around you had Dire Straits, Queen, Phil Collins. These people are great live artists and knew what the concert would do for their careers.' He alleged there were rows about who would get top billing too, and – presumably anticipating this – felt the most obviously selfless act would be to avoid selling his own material altogether. 'I thought that the only real statement I could make was for a white artist to perform three of his favourite black songs,'[24] he said, those being Stevie Wonder's 'Village Ghetto Land', Gladys Knight and the Pips' 'If I Were Your Woman' and Marvin Gaye's 'Sexual Healing' ('which you have to be a hero or a twerp to even attempt',[25] said *NME*'s Stuart Maconie). Admittedly, a big philanthropic display could also backfire, at least as far as your credibility goes. Shortly before *Faith*'s release,

Michael had turned down a spot on the Ferry Aid single – a fundraiser for the victims of the Zeebrugge ferry disaster on 6 March 1987 and their families – because 'I really didn't want to be on the same record as people like Ali from [BBC TV soap opera] *EastEnders*. I'm sorry. If I want to do things for charity I'll do things for charity, but I can't want to make a mockery of my own career musically to do it.'[26] Michael had to mean what he was doing and do it appropriately.

As Paul Gambaccini says, 'The socially conscious side of George was always there. If he gave the proceeds of a single away to charity, he meant it. And as we know, he would send somebody money after he'd heard them on a TV phone-in. This is complete sincerity.' But it also highlights a possible reason why Michael kept his public-spirited deeds under wraps and his politics only implicit. 'It's not fake,' continues Gambaccini, 'but it's also not commercial. Nobody talks about "Hand to Mouth."'

On the contrary, Andy Duncan does. Now a performance coach, on 17 July 1987 – the day he was called into Sarm West Studio 2 to contribute to 'Hand to Mouth' – Duncan was still a percussionist with a bulging list of credits that was halfway through taking in most of 1980s and 1990s pop. Robbie Williams, Kylie and Pet Shop Boys were to come, Linx – alongside 'Wham! Rap' producer Bob Carter – were behind him, and Trevor Horn's ZTT stable of acts was very much in his present. He had also worked on 'Wham! Rap' back in 1982 and remembers Michael having a halting sense of musical direction, yet to match his ambition. 'When we reached the middle section, George said he wanted a drop-out so it just went down to the four-on-the-floor of the bass drum. He asked if I could suggest something to fill that space, so I came up with what became the rhythm part of the whole of that section. What I was interested in as a musician was doing what I call "solving the rhythm puzzle", finding the best way to make it work.'

In July 1987, the rhythm puzzle to solve was reproducing the picture Michael had 'in his mind's ear', to use Duncan's phrase. Chris Porter had called Duncan in – they'd known one another since they were '10 years old; we'd moved to London together and were like brothers' and had of course teamed up on 'Wham! Rap' – and said Michael wanted him to propose some ideas, and they would compare from there. 'I can remember listening to the track,' says Duncan, 'and realizing it had no dynamic drop-out, no big chorus, kind of quiet, just a linear progress through the track. The track sets a mood and the mood is what sustains the song.' The ideas flowed from there. 'There's a clave beat with a big load of reverb on it at the beginning of the track. I said, "Look, if we just put that there, it sets a kind of depth to the sound of the track," and after that I realized, to match its linear feel, it just needed a light touch.'

That light touch naturally brought to mind the triangle, the old fave of the school percussion section. 'Most people get the shivers when you mention it because they remember standing there going "*ting*" every five minutes. It's actually a brilliant rhythm instrument. It sits really well in a mix because it's operating at a frequency level which is not going to be competing with anything else, so you can just park it there. And it adds colour and motion to a track.' Duncan and Michael agreed where the triangle would come in and how the song would have its slow build, but something was missing. 'I said, "I feel like it needs to have a bit of a kick at the end. It needs to change gear ever so slightly." And so we put the bongos in.' Listen from 3:40 for that extra propulsive effect.

The session didn't take too long – 'about three hours maximum,' reckons Duncan. Technical and compositional facts also helped. 'The song was pretty much on the way already,' says Duncan, 'because it's quite a simplistic recording. There's not a lot going on there. And the drum machine was a Linn 9000, not the original LinnDrum. The LinnDrum had certain frustrating limitations around changes of tempo and quantizing [the process that cleans up glitches and inaccuracies in performance]. It was quite crude in terms of how closely you could quantize the notes, but the Linn 9000 was a much more user-friendly bit of gear. When I arrived at Studio 2, there was a guide vocal, the keyboard pad was there and the drums were there. There's not a lot more on the track anyway.' Perhaps slightly more than he first suspected. Looking over an admirably well-kept diary, Duncan finds he'd charged for four overdubs on the track 'so something never made the cull there, or there's something else going on that I can't hear listening back – maybe a shaker'. He also reveals the going rate in 1987 for a percussionist's time and skills: 'My contribution to an album that sold in excess of 25 million copies was worth 300 quid.'

In UK music weekly *Sounds*, Richard Cook was enamoured of the track's – and by extension the whole album's – 'unusual kind of white soul, dry but rich, stark but warm with melody'.[27] *NME*'s Cath Carroll, writing under the alias Myrna Minkoff, heard a 'compassionate, linear croon',[28] while Eleanor Levy, in her album review in another UK weekly, *Record Mirror*, found it 'flows quite nicely', contrasting it with what she felt was the album's overall target, 'a sub-Prince groove which the often quite tinny production fails to transport into the heady realms of the real *groin* music he would seem to be aiming for'.[29] Michael himself recognized its flow and saw how the lyric brought it out, telling *Rolling Stone*, 'the imagery is quite soothing at first. And then if you think about it, it's not at all soothing.'[30] Oddly, 'Hand to Mouth' is more 'Sign "☮"' the Times' than the blatantly Princely 'I Want Your Sex' – in the rhythm of its verses anyway. Perhaps that's the required tempo and timbre for reeling out headlines in songs, a rhetorical tone and relatively little ornamentation, letting the message cut through.

I will be your adult contemporary

John Altman is a composer, arranger and saxophonist, with a career stretching back to the 1950s and a musical lineage that spreads out even further. Two of his uncles – Woolf and Sid Phillips – were bandleaders when big bands and jazz bands were all the rage, pre- and post-war, while Sid's son Simon, Altman's cousin, is a drummer who served time with muscular rock outfits Judas Priest and The Michael Schenker Group and backed legends like Brian Eno, Jeff Beck and Jack Bruce, eventually spending a couple of decades – on and off – behind the kit for AOR monsters Toto. Those are versatile genes, but Altman's own CV puts all that variety in the shade.

Starting off as a kid of just three years old, making good use of family ties by playing with Judy Garland at the Palladium, Altman has belied modest formal training to become a musician who can turn his hand to pretty much anything and rub shoulders with pretty much anyone. His big break was on the road as musical director for the remarkably consistent Brit-soul pioneers Hot Chocolate, before providing similar support for uppity visionary Van Morrison. He's brought the strings to life on Björk's cover of the old big-band jazz-pop standard 'It's Oh So Quiet' and the florid 1988 single 'Hey

Manhattan!' by British perfect pop stalwarts Prefab Sprout and scored endless commercials and plenty of movies. One of his most memorable claims to fame is arranging 'Always Look on the Bright Side of Life', Eric Idle's jaunty, tongue-in-cheek finale to Monty Python's biblical satire *The Life of Brian*. Somewhat improbably, he's also been a musical foil for British drum and bass megastar Goldie, arranging the orchestration for his staggeringly ambitious second album, 1998 breakbeat epic *Saturnz Return*. Though Altman sidestepped the direct glare of the spotlight, it's nevertheless been a glittering career.

But he may have made his greatest cultural impact in the back room of a North London pub in the late 1960s, several years before any of this starry stuff happened. He was a member of a teenage band of future heavyweights called the Ric Parnell Independence, featuring (funnily enough) Atomic Rooster drummer Ric Parnell, who would later meet his fictional maker as Mick Shrimpton in *This Is Spinal Tap*. The rest of the band comprised Ian Dury and the Blockheads guitarist and keyboard player Chaz Jankel, another drummer in Van Morrison session player and future Mike and the Mechanics member Pete Van Hooke and the slightly less celebrated bassist Jon Rose – and they had an unlikely fan. 'You're the reason I took up music,' George Michael told John Altman twenty-eight years later.

The pub where the Ric Parnell Independence practised was called the Railway Hotel – run by Van Hooke's father – and it stood on Station Road in Edgware just across an alleyway from the Angus Pride restaurant. At this stage, around 1969, the Angus Pride was co-owned by Michael's father Jack Panos (the anglicized Kyriacos Panayiotou) and, temporarily at least, he and his young family lived upstairs. Young George would get about. 'We all used to go to George's dad's restaurant,' Altman remembers, 'and apparently he – as a five-year-old – would make a point of coming over to the pub and listening to us rehearse. I don't remember him there, but it clearly stuck with him. What amazes me is how he made the connection. I suppose he eventually learned that Pete's dad owned the place next door, found out who was in the band with Pete Van Hooke, read articles in Van Morrison fanzines, heard me talking about being in a band with Pete and rehearsing in Edgware – and put two and two together!'

Whatever conclusions pinged around Michael's synapses later on, he had other reasons for recruiting Altman initially. 'Kissing a Fool' – the swinging, jazz-tinged finale to *Faith*'s vinyl edition – had been on the back burner for a while, dating back to Wham!'s *Big Tour* of late 1984 and early 1985, but shelved because it blatantly belonged in the solo pot. It wasn't forgotten – in February, Michael was musing over whether it should be 'a Ronnie Scott's type thing or an old-fashioned Nelson Riddle type arrangement'[1] and it was even reportedly the working title[2] for *Faith* before ego and concision prevailed – it just had to be used correctly. Meanwhile, another star of the early 1980s New Pop and synth explosion had been dipping a toe in jazzy waters.

Synth-pop duo Yazoo (Yaz in the United States) had split in 1983 after a quick-fire slew of electronic classics and massive hits couldn't quite bridge the emotional gap between taciturn keyboard boffin Vince Clarke – still smarting from a difficult departure from those other Essex futurists Depeche Mode a couple of years earlier – and rumbustious but extraordinary singer Alison Moyet. Clarke was back within six months, prodding the keys behind former Undertones frontman Feargal Sharkey on short-lived collective The Assembly's UK top five hit 'Never Never'. It was a fair bit longer before Moyet got her act together. When she returned a year on with her first solo single 'Love Resurrection', she was still somewhere near the synth-pop environs, but the song and its album *Alf* had been lavished with a touch more cash than Yazoo had been used to. They had been signed to Mute – a high-profile label that punched above its weight in the chart, but still independent – while Moyet was now music biz royalty on Columbia. *Alf* offered up a trio of moderate hits, 'All Cried Out' and 'Invisible' following 'Love Resurrection' to the also-ran positions on the UK singles chart. It took something a little different to match Yazoo's blockbuster success.

Making hay while the sun shone, however wanly, Columbia requested a fourth single from the album, but Moyet didn't want to short-change the fans so she suggested a curveball, a faithful cover of Billie Holiday's 'That Ole Devil Called Love' which, as Altman tells it, was Moyet's parents' favourite song. It was a far cry from the punchier, flashier singles that preceded it – languid and refined, 'quite a risky move to make',[3] according to Moyet herself, and allowed her enviable pipes to show their subtle side. A huge hit – only 'Easy Lover', Earth, Wind & Fire singer Philip Bailey's premium duet with Phil Collins, denied it a UK number one – 'That Ole Devil Called Love' not only pointed a potential way forward for Moyet (who would dabble again with jazzy archive faves when she recorded the 1940s Oscar nominee 'Love Letters' a couple of years later), it also became a byword for a pop artist branching out and doing something rather more sophisticated. The near future would see the likes of Simply Red and Rick Astley taking it down a notch, following Moyet's lead and digging up the jazz club classics for a patina of urbanity. When George Michael wanted some of that prime real estate for himself, there was an obvious reference point.

While 'Kissing a Fool' was an actual original – not the kind of off-the-peg songbook archetype his contemporaries were picking up – it still needed that lovely oxymoron of an ersatz authentic sheen. It needed to sound like 'That Ole Devil Called Love'. Enter John Altman. 'He phoned me up and the first thing he said to me', Altman recalls, 'was, "I'm doing a track and you're the only person who can do this with me." He knew I'd been involved with "That Ole Devil Called Love", but I deflected him by saying I'd just arranged it, I wasn't the producer. "Yeah," he said, "but we all know who put in all the work." I thought that was quite astute. Up to then I'd only known him as the good-looking guy in Wham!.'

The link between Michael, Altman and the pubs and restaurants of Edgware only came up later, 'out of the blue, somewhere between takes 34 or 35'. From the start though, Michael was clearly prepared to put his trust in the arranger. 'He sent me a demo of "Kissing a Fool,"' says Altman, 'and it was just piano, bass, drum machine and him singing, with no ending to it. "By the time we record, I'll have an ending," he promised, so I booked essentially the same team that was on "That Ole Devil Called Love", guys from my big band. I had Mark Chandler and Steve Waterman on trumpet,

Malcolm Griffiths on trombone, Jamie Talbot on reeds (I was on clarinet and tenor sax, Jamie on clarinet and alto; we switched halfway through the song), Mick Pyne on piano, Hughie Burns was playing guitar – that was George's request, but I loved Hughie anyway – Jeff Clyne on double bass and Ian Thomas on drums.'

This was a first major session for Thomas – who has enjoyed a packed career since, working extensively with Mark Knopfler, Scott Walker, Seal and countless others – and he nearly missed out. Altman approached Pyne and Thomas at the bar during the Edinburgh Jazz Festival. 'I said, "Are you all free on Wednesday to do a session for George Michael?" Apparently, Jeff trod on Ian's foot to stop him saying anything, because he knew he was in the middle of a summer season with Cilla Black. "Yes, we're all free!" It was the first time George and Ian had met, and he became his drummer of choice.'

The 'Kissing a Fool' sessions took place at Sarm West, and another future mainstay of George Michael's inner circle was on board too – keyboard player and backing vocalist Chris Cameron. A Hot Chocolate alumnus like John Altman, Cameron had first come across Michael – and his Wham! partner Andrew Ridgeley – when touring Australia off the back of Hot Chocolate's 1982 smashes 'It Started with a Kiss' and 'Girl Crazy'. 'They were out of their trees,' says Cameron. 'They came into this club in Sydney and ran around all these plants dotted about the place.' Their first semi-formal meeting was a more restrained affair at the now defunct Maison Rouge Studios in Fulham, West London, where Cameron was recording with Icelandic jazz-funkers Mezzoforte and

Michael was working with Wham! producer Steve Brown, 'during the "Wham Rap!" days', as Cameron places it, but more direct involvement came with the Stand By Me AIDS Day Benefit Concert on 1 April 1987 at Wembley Arena in North London, where Michael needed an extra keyboard player. 'He had one in Danny Schogger, who'd been in the National Youth Jazz Orchestra and Hot Chocolate with me,' Cameron adds, inevitably, 'but they needed another and Danny got me the gig.'

He remembers 'Kissing a Fool' as a fully formed song, notwithstanding the brassy crescendo Altman and his band would add later in the sessions. 'How do I know that? Because when he sang it at the microphone – I was on piano – he just sang, there was no lyric sheet. He knew it backwards.' What Michael hadn't mapped out was the arrangement, so while Altman was there for the orchestral touches, Cameron was the man to lay down the chords. 'He'd sing a part and then I'd put chords to it – E minor 7th, G minor, B flat – OK! We'd just do it line by line at the piano. He then went back and did the vocal, because initially we were just trying to get the piano, and then of course they added the drums and bass and John Altman's brass section.'

The big band found Michael clear about what he didn't want. Altman had written out a basic chord chart of his own and Michael asked the horns to duplicate that exactly, and then it was 'take after take, with no indication of why we were redoing it', says Altman. Michael wasn't one for constructive feedback. Eventually, he left them to pack up for the night with no word on whether he was satisfied or disappointed. 'Between recordings we'd been chatting away about the TV dramas I was scoring at the time, but there was never any "Oh, that's a great take – Oh, that's not a great take." I was a bit disconcerted when I got home, so I rang Steve Sidwell and said, "I'm baffled, I'm getting no feedback at all – I don't know if he likes it or hates it." Steve said, "Are you going back?" And I said, "Yes, I'm there tomorrow." "Then he likes it," Steve replied. "Because you'd know soon enough if he didn't." '

For all his apparent reticence, Michael wasn't simply a detached taskmaster, kicking back in the control room, making the musicians play over and over again for the sake of it. He was right there with them. 'We did the rhythm section on the first day,' says Altman, 'and then a couple of days later we went and did the brass, and [Michael] sang every single take in the studio. I was impressed, because I'd never really come across anyone who had that dedication. It was obviously an important song for him.' And the interminable takes? 'I think he was just a perfectionist. As soon as he'd heard what he wanted he was happy.'

So pleased was Michael with the results that – according to Altman – he wasn't interested in getting a band to emulate the arrangement when he took *Faith* on tour. 'I heard he told his touring band, "You're never going to do it as well as these guys did," so he played a tape instead.' Altman and his cohorts did, however, get an opportunity to recreate the performance themselves – in mime anyway. 'I was recording a commercial at Advision [Studios – now known as The Sound Company, based in Fitzrovia, Central London, just north of Oxford Street], where Wham! recorded "Last Christmas", and I got a call from George's management asking if the band and I could be on set on Thursday or Friday to do the "Kissing a Fool" video, the Musicians' Union rule being if you're on the record they can't use anyone else. I got them to cancel their commitments, the usual palaver. Five hours later, I rang the office back and said, "Success! I've got everybody. Isn't that wonderful?" And they told me, "Oh, George has changed his mind. He wants to do it on Monday." So I gave them the numbers and left them to sort it out themselves. Of course, the video's full of male models and hip-looking guys from his usual band – not this bunch of balding, overweight jazz musicians.'

Altman and Michael would bump into each other in the intervening years, and while fond words were exchanged, it didn't lead to any further collaboration. Chris Cameron, on the other hand, was set to stick around, and 'Kissing a Fool' stands out for him because of how unusual it was to find Michael arriving in the studio with a largely complete song. 'The typical form was, you'd play four bars and then go and sit outside while George twiddled around with it for a while, maybe came up with a melody line. Then you'd come back in after a couple of hours to do another four bars, and on it went. When we were doing *Faith*, I used to bring other arranging work with me, because you were never going to play a whole song in two or three takes and then go. No, you'd sit there for hours and only play 16 bars.' Cameron would get used to the process. 'I never did another session with George like "Kissing a Fool" until we recorded "Patience" 15 years later. Otherwise, he nearly always wrote in the studio. That's just how he liked to work.' And Cameron's next major input was a pure studio creation.

If 'Kissing a Fool' is ostensibly George Michael trying his hand at voguish jazz-club sophistication, it also has a timeless quality. These things come around time and again, the cool reborn and reborn. *Faith* isn't just a very 1987 attempt at global domination, it's a showcase for songs that are set to endure. In its appropriation of tried and tested poses, 'Kissing a Fool' knows it has an afterlife. The title track too. The more obviously 'now' songs, the post-Prince funk-outs 'Hard Day', 'I Want Your Sex' and 'Monkey' aren't built for that purpose; they're not trying to get into the Adult Contemporary songbook like 'Kissing a Fool' or 'Father Figure' – or 'One More Try'.

Not that 'One More Try' was a strategic, precisely manufactured strike at the pantheon. It was plucked from the fire. 'I actually wrote the whole thing from start to finish in eight hours,'[4] Michael told *No.1* magazine on the release of the album. 'We recorded it the same day. I was working on another song which was going disastrously then this just came out.'

Cameron remembers its roots. 'We were working on another song; it wasn't in 3 like "One More Try". Anyway, we took a break and I started fooling around, playing a couple of old Spinners ballads that have that descending chord structure "One More Try" shares. I loved the Spinners, Thom Bell, the Stylistics, that whole Gamble & Huff thing – and you can hear that. One of them was "I Could Never (Repay Your Love)" from *Spinners* (1973) – their first album on Atlantic – and the other was "Love Don't Love Nobody" from the follow-up, *Mighty Love* (1974).' Something made Michael prick up his ears. 'Both songs have that churchy vibe,' says Cameron, 'that feel when you walk down the aisle. George turned around for a second and said, "What's that?" I started to work with it, changing it around a little, and that's how it began. He listened for a while, then said, "Oh, play that again." I played it in a slightly different way and he went, "No, you didn't do that last time, you did *that*. You went *there*." So he was actually listening, and that's how "One More Try" started.' 'Levi Jeans soul',[5] *Q*'s Chris Heath called it, noticing shared ambience with Percy Sledge's 'When a Man Loves a Woman', which featured on a famous Levi's commercial earlier that year.

The 'rhapsodic ballad'[6] was constructed quickly from Cameron's starting point. 'George was trying to keep it as limited as possible,' says Chris Porter, lead engineer throughout the *Faith* sessions. 'As simple and unflowery as possible.' It all came together far more quickly than Chris Cameron expected. 'I thought we were doing a bloody demo! Because the organ you hear isn't a Hammond, it's a Roland Juno-60 [the same model is played on 'A Different Corner'] and the strings are a Yamaha DX7 and another Roland synth that was just lying around the studio.' That was back at Puk Studios, in Jutland, Denmark, where musicians were coming and going during that period. By the time Cameron returned a week later, the song had moved on considerably. 'Muggins here thinks we're going to redo the Juno-60 parts with a proper Hammond organ, get a real rhythm section and I'm going to write up some strings and it's all going to be wonderful. But it was a finished record! It didn't need real strings or a real organ.'

Chris Porter remembers some adornment. 'Ian Thomas played drums on the track, a very simple drum pattern, but this was one of his very early sessions and, looking at the studio notes, I see that we've got his kit but we've added quite a lot to it – new bass drum, new toms, new riser. It wasn't a lack in his playing ability. It would have been for dramatic effect.'

In any case, Michael had pulled out the lyrics and nailed the vocals almost within minutes of Cameron establishing the basic chords a week earlier. 'I heard the vocal and I was gobsmacked at how brilliant it was,' Cameron marvels, years later. 'Left to his own devices, he just went with how he felt, and I admired that.' Leaving Michael to work at his own pace – whether it was lightning fast or in painstaking segments – seems to have been key. 'I've seen some musicians try to give him input', says Cameron. 'Really good musicians, but it's a misjudgement. They were *gone*. You had to be patient. When it's right, it's right, and like I say, sometimes you'd come back after you'd done something you thought was just ordinary – and you'd hear the vocal and go, "Fucking hell. Where did that come from?"'

His vocals were transformative enough to make a gem of unremarkable material – 'His range was sensational,' as Cameron has it – but the reason they really soared was down to sincerity. The earthy, soul-rending pleas of 'One More Try' aren't performative; Michael's wrenching them from his very core. 'It was his whole feel,' Cameron continues. 'George always wrote about what was going on in his life, so what he was singing about he felt with every sinew of his body. That's what people connect with. The content of his lyrics came from his heart, and "One More Try" is a perfect example of that.' In the *No.1* feature, Michael suggests it's the same heart that was so lovesick on 'A Different Corner', although here he's 'decided'[7] the fate of the relationship. The implication is it's Pat Fernandes – model, close friend and sometime assistant of the singer – who is the subject both times, and the two were regularly photographed together and often said to be dating in the mid-1980s. Seventeen years later, Michael admitted to *GQ* magazine that make-up artist Kathy Jeung, star of the 'I Want Your Sex' video, was the only girlfriend he ever really had, and she knew he was bisexual.[8] Any or all of these positions are just about compatible with each other, naturally. Whatever, he's leaving this chapter of his life behind, begging to be freed, a favourite state of his.

With its heavily stylized sex scene, 'Father Figure' was another video to get Michael into trouble – 'We cut out a couple of scenes with the model wearing black suspenders,'[9] said a spokesperson for *The Roxy*, ITV's short-lived rival to the BBC's *Top of the Pops* – but above all, it was a mini-film to show where the oodles of cash were starting to go. 'It was my first big shoot in LA,' director Andy Morahan told the *Young Director Award*. 'There was no performance and just narrative. I felt like a big shot Hollywood director!'[10] Michael's off his knees for the song itself, where the protagonist is dominant, offering an escape route. Here's the big honest guy you can rely on. There's still a certain amount of insecurity in the pleas to be understood but hip-grinding confidence with it. And then there's the 'sex clap'. The what? 'The "sex clap"', says Chris Porter. 'We put down a LinnDrum pattern and then, instead of using the snare, we triggered what we called the "sex clap". The LinnDrum sounded too heavy for what was coming.' The 'sex clap' was an example of early sampling techniques. 'Things were changing very fast,' remembers

Porter. 'Engineers were using some of the first samplers, and I know there were Fairlights about, but we didn't have one of those and we didn't have a Synclavier. We were using a very early British sampling device called a Greengate DS:3, and "Father Figure" is where it really comes in.' Removing the snare changed the tempo and the whole feel of the song. 'The "sex clap" was just some claps we'd sampled from some track or other. It's the finger clicks that are the majority of the backbeat and the "sex clap" is sucked up into those pops with that ridiculous, non-linear, delayed reverb on it. You get a kickback. That wasn't an accident.'

The Greengate isn't the only brand spanking new equipment on 'Father Figure', as Chris Cameron points out. 'Faith is full of Roland D-50. That was the new synth and it was everywhere. I mean, listen to "Father Figure"'s Middle Eastern motif – that's a stock D-50 sound. I play the D-50 regularly on the album – along with Rhodes piano and clavinet – but not on "Father Figure". That was George.' The cold machines and their young, raw master construct a dank, mysterious atmosphere, a kind of foreboding that's swept aside by a redemptive chorus.

Hands-on as ever, Michael was particularly attentive with his vocals on 'Father Figure', and it was Chris Porter's job to interpret his instructions – however esoteric – and ensure reproduction was immediate. 'The vocals were very carefully constructed,' he says. 'They weren't one-take wonders by any means. We spent a lot of time in front of the microphone, literally, and we didn't rely on editing. We were creating it by having George sing, dropping him in, listening back then saying, "Let's get that phrase again, let's get that word again," and starting over.' It seems very little of the vocal presentation was down to post-production. Instead, it was organically inauthentic – a kind of enhanced realism. 'You see, George would always sing in the studio with all the effects we were likely to put on,' explains Porter. 'So, for instance, on "Father Figure" there's a delay on the vocal and he'd say, "Right, I need to hear that delay as I'm singing, so that I can make sure my timing makes the delay sound good," or vice versa.'

Often it was more complex than that, with Michael wanting 'the reverb to be "like glass" – shimmering and popping off', setting Porter the kind of challenge on which he thrived. 'We'd create this whole environment for him to do his vocal before he even started, so he'd go up to the mic and perhaps say, "I need a bit more top" or "I need to hear that delay less" or "I need that close delay a bit louder", and then he'd sing into that, so it's almost sculpting the vocal into the effects we'd set up.' And Porter and his team (including assistant engineers Paul Gomersall and Paul Wright) would hear an instruction to make the vocal sound 'like glass' and know exactly how to achieve this. 'Sure, we didn't have that many tools in order to do it – in some cases only a Lexicon L480 [reverb console released in 1986] – but I had settings I knew would work for that kind of thing. After that you just adjust the dials.' Porter had a strong sense of what worked for Michael, and it's still fresh in his mind. 'He loved it when his "s"s and "t"s zinged off the plate and into the distance, so you'd take the low-mid range out of the plate or digital reverb and extend the length of the treble decay. You'd add some pre-delay too, so the vocal sounds right up close, but everything is happening behind it.' Porter admits it wasn't a new technique by any means. Even so, the distinct, tight – and yes, glassy – vocal sound is very George Michael, but vaguely reminiscent of contemporaneous work by Peter Gabriel, another former singer of a hugely successful band, now shipping unimaginable quantities of albums and taking a keen interest in studio trickery. There's something in stamping your personality on a record – every click, every breath – once you have no one else to worry about.

However idiosyncratic the lead vocal, there's another singer credited on 'Father Figure', the sole time this happens on *Faith*. That's not to say no one else backs Michael up – there's a claim on 'Hard Day', as we'll see – but only Shirley Lewis gets her name in print.

Lewis is steeped in music. Her younger sister Dee enjoyed a clutch of minor hits in the late 1980s at around the time Shirley was flirting with solo chart success, but it's her older sister Linda who greased the wheels for her. Folk-soul singer Linda Lewis's continuing career stretches back to the 1960s and peaked with a UK top 10 cover of Betty Everett's 'The Shoop Shoop Song (It's in His Kiss)' – simply released as 'It's in His Kiss' – in 1975. Born Linda Fredericks, she took the name Lewis to avoid being confused with her labelmate, the singer and stage actress Linda Kendrick, and somehow the new name appended itself to her sisters too. 'Linda used to take me to sessions with her when I was young – the first ever session I did was with Manfred Mann, would you believe? – and people automatically assumed my surname was Lewis,' says Shirley Lewis. 'That's what they called me when they booked me in for my own sessions.'

After a handful of tours with her older sister, Lewis found her own niche – singing and touring with some of the UK's biggest acts, notably new romantics turned blustery balladeers Spandau Ballet, and Elton John. Both would be instrumental in opening new doors for her. 'I first met George at Live Aid [13 July 1985], when I was performing with Spandau Ballet,' she says, 'and then I went off on tour with Elton, and George came along too because they were doing a video for Elton's [1985 UK and US top 20 hit single] "Wrap Her Up."' Michael clearly took a shine to Lewis, suggesting she work with him once she was off the tour. 'At that point, I didn't know if it would be a Wham! album or whatever.' A little while after Lewis completed her commitment to Elton John, she received a call from Michael in June 1987 asking her to come down to Sarm West. It turned out to be a real feather in the cap. 'At the time, he didn't use a lot of singers,' Lewis says. 'Obviously with Wham! he used to do his own backing vocals, so it was really interesting that he'd decided to use back-up for *Faith*. It was a big honour to be asked, especially as the only female on the album.'

When Lewis arrived at Sarm, Michael was 'literally writing ['Father Figure''s] bridge section. The song wasn't finished at all.' Working on the fly as usual, he had also called Lewis at very short notice, leaving her no time to find a babysitter for her three-year-old daughter Carli. 'She just sat outside the room with her colouring books. Looking back now, having my daughter there too makes it even more special.'

As beloved a memory as it is, Lewis's time in the studio with Michael was as fragmented as everyone else's. 'Father Figure' was in fact very far from being finished and Lewis needed to be on her toes to help complete each section. 'I was there all afternoon because he was writing the song as we went along, occasionally saying, "OK, I've got this bit coming: I sing this and we do that ... " and then I'd have to wait for another two hours until he was finally ready to do the chorus.' During Michael's periods of reflection, Lewis would nip out of the studio to spend time with her daughter, each displaying exemplary patience until Carli eventually fell asleep.

Rob Kahane, Michael's manager at the time, has a rather less tolerant view of the singer's disjointed approach to 'Father Figure'. Although based in the United States, he was in the UK for much of the Sarm West *Faith* sessions. 'I was at Sarm forever,' he confirms. 'I hated it. I mean, I liked watching George put his songs together, but – I remember this from "Father Figure" – this is the way he records: he'll put down the first verse and then he needs to go drive his car. He could only write while he was moving, so he either wrote on planes, trains or in cars. He couldn't write sitting still, for whatever reason; he needed to be moving. And, you know, he was writing brilliant songs – nobody was going to stop him from moving. So, I'd arrive at Sarm, jetlagged, and say, "Where's George?" "Oh, he's driving." And he could be driving for, like, four, five fucking hours. Then he'd come back, do a few things and go off driving again. It was a long, tedious process.'

Shirley Lewis kept her head in the game, enjoying being on call. She believes her privileged position as the only other (credited) singer on *Faith* was down to a particular quality Michael enjoyed about her vocals. 'There's a part of my voice that is very breathy,' she says, 'and he liked that. Of course, I also had a knack of being able to emulate his voice – maybe what he really liked is that I sounded like him! I just found it easy to match his tone, and perhaps he was drawn to a voice that paired with his yet was female. But that breathiness – we used to do a lot of tracks and a good deal of them used to be just breath. It's not easy to do, but I just happened to have the ability and George really liked that.' It's another expression of that up-close feel Michael wanted Chris Porter to capture over and over again.

Having only recorded the vocal exchanges on the bridge that first afternoon, Lewis had no idea how the final song would turn out. She was back at Sarm the next day to work on the choruses, where she and Michael would really find out how their voices intertwined. 'George wanted it to sound like a choir,' Lewis remembers, 'so we did a lot of singing the same melody and harmonies. Obviously, as the melody got higher, it wasn't good for his voice, so I did the higher parts and he took the lower.' Lewis can vouch for Michael wanting to hear all the effects that would be put on his voice as he went along. 'That was really important to him, not doing it dry. They would still enhance it in the mix, but he did like a certain amount of delay in the room.'

When Lewis and Michael meshed on the 'Father Figure' chorus, it came out pure gospel. 'I'm not even sure if he was really prepared for that,' says Lewis. 'But once I got in there, he played up to it.' The gospel effect delighted Michael so much, he went for it again three years later on 'Freedom 90', the second track on *Faith*'s follow-up *Listen Without Prejudice Vol. 1*, featuring Shirley Lewis once more. The comeback established her as a fixture of the George Michael team and she would tour and record with him right up until his final album release *Symphonica* in 2014 (largely recorded live on tour in 2011/12). 'Every time we performed "Father Figure" in rehearsal, he'd say, "That's just me and you, Shirl, isn't it?" He always said it.'

'Freedom 90' had been a return from the cold for Lewis because she had been unable to join the *Faith* tour in the whirlwind year after the album was released. 'It's one of the regrets of my life,' she says now. 'George told me he was doing a tour and he'd really love me to come on it, but I'd just signed a solo deal with A&M Records and had a commitment there.' It must have been torture for Lewis when she was ably replaced for the *Faith* gigs by Lynn Mabry, but she believes in a kind of destiny that habitually brought her back to Michael. 'You have a path in life, and refusing that tour – well, normally that would've been it, but it was fate that George came back to me for *Listen Without Prejudice*. And again, when I had to leave the *Cover to Cover* tour in 1991 to go back to my daughter, he still called me up for *25 Live*, 15 years later.'

But maybe that's not providence; maybe it's just talent. Lewis remains grateful. 'I've been on a lot of George's albums, but I have more affection for *Faith* because I feel like he was this huge star, it was his first solo album, he could've used any singer in the world and he didn't – he chose me.'

The memory Paul Gomersall can't shift dates back to the song's early steps at Puk Studios. 'We'd got the backing track together during the day, and the moments when George feels like singing are sporadic,' he says. Even so, studio forays in the middle of the night were still rare. 'It was two in the morning and George just went in there and belted it out. Chris and I went, "Wow." There was one bit – I shouldn't really say, but there was one bit of the song that couldn't be repeated. That top note. It was magical. For me it was one of those magical moments and only Chris and I witnessed it. I can just hear it coming out of the speakers. He could never hit that top note again, so we had to try and sample it. It was beautiful.'

Those instances were so precious because Michael worked quickly when he was in the zone. Gomersall remembers Wham!'s 'Wake Me Up Before You Go-Go' being recorded and mixed in half a day, 'Father Figure''s backing track and pre-Shirley Lewis vocals written and finalized in a day and night, 'One More Try' effectively invented and laid down in a couple of hours. 'He'd stuff up and go back on things,' admits Gomersall, 'and if Chris or I heard something wrong that George hadn't noticed – he had incredible ears, but sometimes we'd spot things – we'd sort it, normally after he'd gone home. Nothing worse than stopping a session so an engineer can fix something. It's a real vibe killer.' Michael just wanted to move on. 'When you worked with George,' Gomersall adds, 'he was all, "Let's get the rhythm track finished so we can start on the vocals." He was happy to get it done.' Don't worry about the technical stuff, just turn out the classics.

Bearing the crossover

By 1986, Wham! had left their contemporaries and supposed rivals gasping. Duran Duran had split into art house and lumpen funk-rock factions, Arcadia and The Power Station failing to add flair or significant hits to the brand before half the band returned later in the year to half the fans. Culture Club were hobbled by the twin evils of Boy George's heroin addiction and a well of inspiration that had dried right up – the two issues presumably related. Spandau Ballet's increasingly flimsy songs couldn't carry the weight of burgeoning visual and musical opulence. Even Frankie Goes to Hollywood, who had looked like the fiercest competition just twelve months earlier, were discovering their intra-band camaraderie was too weak to glue them together once the initial boom had bust, and they didn't make sense if they weren't number one. Only a-ha and Tears for Fears looked as if they could just about hold their own in a hit parade slugfest. It was still early days for the Norwegian trio, though, while the west country Janovians Tears for Fears, who had looked impregnable in the summer of 1985 when their portentous second album *Songs from the Big Chair* was enjoying a month at the head of *Billboard*'s Top Pop Albums, were about to hunker down for three years of squabbling and occasional jazz-hued proggy workouts before their third album *Seeds of Love* blew the budget and their partnership. Basically, George Michael and Andrew Ridgeley had conquered everyone else and now they were vanquishing themselves.

Away from the constraints of the group, Michael was free to pursue all sorts of new directions. It was time to go for that triple crown shared by Madonna, Prince and Michael Jackson. On the release of *Faith* in October 1987 – two months after Jackson had put out *Bad* – Michael told *No.1* magazine, 'Obviously a lot of people are seeing *Faith* as direct competition to *Bad* but I think they're very different albums. Mine relies much more on different musical ideas while his is selling a particular lifestyle – BAD – a particular personality.'[1] Addressing the other two in the triumvirate, he told British journalist Tony Parsons, 'I will never be in step with Madonna or Prince because they are pretty much the people they portray themselves to be. I think I am capable of blanketing the planet because my music is good enough to do it. But unlike Madonna or Prince, I have to become someone else when I do it.'[2] For a man dismissing parallels, he was giving them a lot of thought.

To face Prince and Jackson, Michael would have to meet them on their own ground, America's R&B/Black music market – which is exactly where he wanted to be. He already had the power and depth to be the best white soul singer of his generation, so why not take that a step further? It would be a divisive move. Gingerly testing the solo waters again with 'A Different Corner' in March 1986, three months before Wham!'s official split, Michael was still working within the

'Careless Whisper' palette – refined, delicate, essentially blue-eyed, those feet rooted to the spot. He needed to find some rhythm. It was a slow process, but he'd been making moves towards acceptance by Black audiences for some time.

The most significant early overture had taken place in spring 1985, shortly after Wham!'s celebrated yet bizarre short tour of China. The legendary Apollo Theater in Harlem, New York City, was reopening after one of several rounds of renovations over the years, and toasting its near half-century with a six-hour concert on 4 May featuring many of the greats of Black American music from its lifetime, to raise money for Africare, the Ethiopian Famine Relief Fund. It was nominally a showcase for Motown Records and its own crop of superstars, including Smokey Robinson, Diana Ross, Stevie Wonder and The Four Tops, but also featured Al Green, Patti Labelle, Wilson Pickett and, to broaden the global reach of the NBC TV special (hosted by comedian Bill Cosby and airing on 19 May), a clutch of white singers, led by crossover performers Joe Cocker, Rod Stewart – and George Michael. Cocker and Stewart had form between them as habitual cover artists of Marvin Gaye, Sam Cooke, The Isley Brothers, Otis Redding and more. Michael was more of an unknown quantity in this company but, after a botched first chorus, Wham! co-manager Simon Napier-Bell was impressed to see that Michael had the self-possession to stop the band and give 'Careless Whisper' another go – and the audience recognized game when they saw it. 'Amazingly, before he started singing they burst into applause,' Napier-Bell said. 'He sang as well as I'd ever heard him sing ... the audience burst into more applause, almost drowning out his singing.'[3] He had a modest bit of help in the latter part of the song, with Motown royalty Robinson joining him to sing the second verse and chorus and stick around for a few ad libs, and enjoyed an equally glamorous collaboration on his next number. 'I was asked … were there any other artists that I would like to work with from Motown?' Michael told *Smash Hits* magazine at the end of 1986. 'At which my eyes lit up and I said, "Stevie Wonder", thinking there would be no chance of doing it.'[4] The pair delivered a mutual favourite, Wonder's own 'Love's in Need of Love Today' from classic double album *Songs in the Key of Life* (1976), upholding a lasting Michael trend of performing Wonder covers at any given moment, and went down a storm. 'It was a kind of black acceptance for Wham!,' Michael added. He would carry that with him.

Pop don and broadcaster Paul Gambaccini says, 'George was accepted by Black people as far back as "Careless Whisper". Ray Parker Jr. shaking his head was indicative of what was to come.' Indeed, three Wham! hits had made the *Billboard* Hot Black singles chart, 'Careless Whisper' (credited, as we've seen, to Wham! featuring George Michael) outstripping the more naturally R&B likes of 'Everything She Wants' and 'I'm Your Man' with a number eight peak in March 1985. For Gambaccini though, the real appeal was much more basic than any lyrical acumen. 'He was a very soulful singer. I mean, if your heroes of the 1970s are Stevie Wonder, The Isley Brothers and Elton John, there's a lot of soul in there.' The latter has some resonance here as a sometime effective crossover artist. Mary J. Blige – who, if we're wrapping everything up neatly in a bow, duetted with

Michael on a cover of Wonder's 'As' in 1999 – was apparently asked why she had made a record with Elton John (a version of John's own 'I Guess That's Why They Call It the Blues', which appears on her 2006 album *Mary J. Blige & Friends*, and in live form on John's *Elton John – One Night Only – The Greatest Hits*) and leapt to the old piano man's defence. 'She said she refused to have anything bad said about Elton,' recounts Gambaccini, 'because when she was young, her father played Elton John "and he brought happiness to our home."' The way Gambaccini views it, that torch was passed on. 'George also brought happiness to a lot of Black people. Does the audience recognize an isolated voice in pain? I think soul is recognized whoever it's from.' At his core, Michael may have been a natural fit for crossover. 'I grew up with American black music,' he told *Life* in September 1988, 'and I've become a musician who does a form of soul music that is accepted by American black people and by musicians.'[5] In his head, he was making it happen.

Beyond the Motown anniversary show, Stevie Wonder was pencilled in to play an even more substantial role in Michael's wooing of Black record buyers soon after Wham!'s final gig. This would be the prestige duet to propose Michael's place in the US big league before his debut solo album seconded it, but as Michael's then-manager Rob Kahane says, 'Stevie Wonder never turned up to the studio to record it, on two different occasions.' The honour famously fell to a soul legend of equal status – Aretha Franklin – but somewhere in between even Whitney Houston was in the mix. As Napier-Bell tells it, Houston arrived at the 13th Annual American Music Awards (27 January 1986) with Arista Records boss and all-round music biz Midas Clive Davis, and Davis approached Napier-Bell's business partner Jazz Summers to suggest a team-up between his overnight sensation and the hungry Michael. Summers was hungrier still and immediately upgraded to Franklin – in his mind, at least. He played along in present company.

Michael himself remembers being approached to write for Franklin as far back as 1984, when 'Careless Whisper' was turning heads everywhere, and shying away from such an awesome challenge. 'It shocked me,' he told MTV in 1988. 'Aretha to me is the best female soul artist in the world, and even though I was a confident individual and we'd started having really big hits . . . it was just frightening.'[6] Whatever the chronology, whoever had the lightbulb moment first, it all came together around eighteen months later, and this time, having more than stood his ground alongside Smokey and Stevie, Michael knew he could not only inhabit the same studio as Aretha, he was ready to sing with her too. Bringing some Atlantic soul to Motown, 'I Knew You Were Waiting (For Me)' was co-written by Simon Climie (who had just joined forces with Rob Fisher as briefly successful British pop-soul duo Climie Fisher) and Nashville session player Dennis Morgan – and was recorded in Detroit. It was still remembered fondly by Franklin after Michael's death thirty years later, reminding her of cuts she used to record back in the day with Jerry Wexler, when they would discover the magic by sleeping on a new song and seeing if they still liked it in the morning. 'Musically, it does not grow old,'[7] she told *Entertainment Weekly*. While you'd be loath to argue with the Queen of Soul, it's very much a late 1980s confection, Narada

Michael Walden's production huge and expensive sounding, but the committed performances and infectious sense of euphoria pull it through.

And of course, the whole project was mutually beneficial. Michael needed his cred, Franklin could see no harm in appealing to this generation's pop kids and got her first UK number one hit into the bargain.

But it's all very well duetting with your favourite artists on your favourite songs, or having a vocal face-off to something out of the Climie hit factory. To really step into the arena, Michael needed to write convincing R&B and front it out as well. 'I Want Your Sex' – his first tilt at Prince's territory, as we've seen, and first single free of the Wham! day job – was a move in that direction, but as *Spin* reported, Black radio refused to play the song. 'It's the worst reaction I've had on a record for years,' Michael said in an interview with the magazine later in 1987. 'For them it was too dirty.'[8] Most frustratingly for Michael, he felt the single was 'perhaps the most successfully black-sounding record I've ever done. Having spent a lot of time listening to modern black music and dancing in clubs, that song is my reflection of my life at the moment.'[9] He needed to reach beyond the scandal and drive that lance home. On 'Hard Day' he does just that – again, with a whisper of inspiration from Prince and, later, with a dance floor boost from New York remixer du jour Shep Pettibone.

It's one of *Faith*'s two 'auteur' tracks (alongside the first part – 'Rhythm 1: Lust' of 'I Want Your Sex'), where Michael is credited with 'Vocals/all instruments', although regular keyboard player Chris Cameron remembers it slightly differently: 'I sang on "Hard Day", doing the bass voice because George wanted another side, not just him.' Cameron also recalls adding 'the string synth on the bridge, where it changes from the E flat minor funky thing to the B section', but is phlegmatic about credits. 'There were rarely Musicians' Union forms around in those days. And I think George used to get the hump sometimes if they happened to be there and we were signing them, so they were lackadaisical about them. But that was pop.'

On 'Hard Day', credit is due, again – at least in part – to Prince. 'George had spent a fair bit of time by this point in the States,' says Chris Porter. 'He'd worked with Narada Michael Walden, so he knew the kind of musician who worked on tracks like this, and he was heavily influenced by Prince. He'd been listening to a lot of Prince stuff and Prince inspired – particularly on "Faith", the single – that kind of dry, upfront vocal sound. It changed the way we thought about vocals. That was definitely because George had been exposed to these people while he'd been out in the States. And in the mind of his management, there was certainly a feeling that he needed to do more out there.' Rob Kahane is clear on just how difficult this has always been. 'There's so much competition in [the United States] for airplay at the right radio stations, for MTV play at that time, for the right press – you're competing against so many other superstars that the space is limited. And if you're a British artist signed to a British record label and you're coming to America, the Americans are making less money than the British are making, so their incentive to work with you is decreased.'

As for the recording techniques involved in 'Hard Day', although it's easy to draw a direct parallel between the apparently pitched-up vocals at its close and, say, Prince performing as alter ego Camille on 'If I Was Your Girlfriend' from *Sign "☮" the Times*, crucially released in the middle of the *Faith* sessions, Porter insists they weren't going for a facsimile. 'I didn't know how [Prince] was doing it, but mostly it's irrelevant what someone else does with various effects because every voice is different, every song is different. We just experimented until we got a sound that we liked. Getting the Prince sound in general is really a very tight digital delay and lots of compression.' Porter wasn't sticking Michael's head in a soundproof box for the starkest sound possible, but they would have, he says, 'made a vocal booth to tighten up the sound even in a small room. Sarm 2, for instance, is a fairly small live space, probably only 20 square metres – it's quite a dead room – but even then we would've tightened that up more with a vocal booth. We didn't have reflection filters, which I use a lot nowadays to get a really nice, tight, close vocal sound.'

Despite not knowing precisely how Prince was getting into vocal character for Camille, Porter had his own methods. 'We would have varisped the whole thing down as far as we could – you could varispeed a Mitsubishi 32-track recorder down by up to 10 per cent, so we would probably have gone down the full 10 per cent, recorded the vocal normally and then sped it up.'

'Monkey' is in a similar vein – hard, electro-seasoned R&B whipcracking its way to the dance floor. There's a go-go element to this one; it could keep its end up alongside contemporary smashes from Cleveland's The Dazz Band, Sacramento's Club Nouveau and NYC's Cameo – not that their frontman Larry Blackmon would be wild about the idea. In a *Rolling Stone* interview earlier in the year, he dismissed Michael and other white superstars dabbling in R&B – Steve Winwood, Peter Gabriel – as 'guys who are "trying to be funky"',[10] presumably to no avail. Still, 'Monkey' fits Michael's floor-filling intentions, even if it's almost an afterthought. Although it's just Michael and guitarists Robert Ahwai and Roddy Matthews playing on the track, Chris Cameron remembers its last-minute gestation. Quite simply, 'George said, "I need another uptempo song," and we were all – not exactly struggling, but thinking, "Come on, come on, come on."'

While he doesn't play on the finished track, Cameron's got a feeling for 'Monkey''s origins because *Faith*'s final piece in the jigsaw was initially going in another direction, and he was there. With a peerless grasp on events from more than thirty years ago and a bracing willingness to give up confidences, guitarist Roddy Matthews – now a songwriting tutor at the London College of Creative Media with decades of composition for film and TV, as well as an eclectic history of session work, behind him – picks up the story. 'I got a call from Sarm West saying, "Chris Porter wants you to play on a George Michael session," which was quite a big deal for me. It was a Sunday in September 1987, and George Michael was in my life for five days.'

A chain of connections had brought Matthews to Sarm West. Former Wham! backing vocalists Helen 'Pepsi' DeMacque and Shirlie Holliman – Pepsi & Shirlie, to give

them their pop-star sobriquet – had come flying out of the
blocks after the break-up and turned up in the UK top 10
in January 1987 with debut single 'Heartache' just as their
ex-boss was hitting the top of the tree with Aretha Franklin.
The new duo's follow-up single 'Goodbye Stranger', released
in May, was – like 'Heartache' – co-written and produced
by Tambi Fernando, this time alongside Pete Hammond,
mixmaster at PWL (Pete Waterman Limited), the self-
styled 'Hit Factory' owned by Pete Waterman of the wildly
successful Stock Aitken Waterman production partnership –
a colossus bestriding the UK singles chart in the closing years
of the 1980s. Hammond brought in his friend Roddy to play
some funky licks. 'It changed my life,' says Matthews. 'When
you've played on a hit record, there's an aura about you which
is entirely undeserved. People expect you to be a talisman.'
Matthews was subsequently called back in for other songs
Fernando was working on, and one happened to have Chris
Porter sitting in as co-producer.

That first Sunday in September, George Michael was barely
in Roddy Matthews' life at all. Matthews, Chris Cameron, Deon
Estus and drummer Ian Thomas stayed in the Sarm reception
as 'George walked in and went straight into the studio. We
heard drum machine noises for three hours and then he
left.' The next day, Matthews waited at home until 4.00 p.m.
before calling Michael's management to see if he was
required. 'Whoever answered said, "No, he's driving around
in his car, trying to come up with something."' George was in
his thinking place. Picture Rob Kahane swearing in the lobby.

Things picked up for Matthews on Tuesday. 'I got a call
saying, "Yeah, he's on to something – can you bring your

12-string?" They're an absolute motherfucker to play. You can't do it for hours and hours because it just kills you. Anyway, I sat down with a tuner and George goes to Chris Cameron, "OK, the first chord is [sings rising notes], the second chord is [more sung notes], the third chord is [lower notes]" – he sang the chords!' Matthews had never seen anyone do this, but Michael had got it absolutely right. 'Chris [Cameron] has perfect pitch, so he wrote it out: B Minor, E, G; then called out a tempo and we started playing.'

Otherwise, Michael wasn't singing at all. 'He just listened,' says Matthews. 'It's all going on in his head.' As the musicians ran it through a third time, he walked out of the room, but they carried on. After a few minutes, one of the studio staff told them Michael had left in his car. 'He's got us here like a human jukebox,' laughs Matthews. 'He hasn't even switched us off.' Whatever his bewilderment, Matthews took certain insights from his time with Michael, spotting the talent in the quirks. 'He was a genius naïf. He didn't know what he was doing, but it worked in a way that people who know more can't get to. He wrote remarkably good melodies for someone who couldn't play an instrument, very bright, major key melodies. Diatonic would be the technical word.' It's, inevitably, an enduring mystery. 'I don't know how he visualized music. It must have been very odd, and that makes him a kind of genius. The fact he was able to do so much . . . picturing.'

It's Wednesday. Nothing happens. Thursday, nothing. 'All I'm doing is sitting at home waiting for a call, doing my ironing. I'm on a £400-a-day ironing job for George Michael. Also, all my equipment's there – I've got two or three guitars, two amplifiers, a pile of stuff. Eventually, I crack at 2.00 p.m. and ring up, scared they've found someone else. And all they say is I can come and collect my gear. I'm crestfallen; all that work and I've been sacked. But this is where it gets lucky.' Michael's solution is to dig up the bones of a track he'd started at Puk, and, with Sarm booked for a couple of weeks, he's getting on with it. 'Disappointed, I got the tube over to Sarm at about 4.00 p.m.,' continues Matthews. 'I went into the small studio to sort out my gear and the tape op came in and said, "He's had an idea. Unpack your guitar." If I hadn't been there, who knows what would have happened?'

Mercifully, the 12-string was not required this time around. Instead, Matthews got to use his 'session' guitar, a Japanese ESP Stratocaster with active pickups. That said, there was another physical challenge for the Matthews fingers when Michael told him what he was looking for. 'It was bloody hard. He played me what he had of the song so far, and then said, "I want you to play [sings the twanging stanza punctuation from the 'Monkey' verses]." I played it back straight with a pick, but he said, "Not that, *this*," emphasizing the bend in the final note of the lick. Now, that's really difficult. There's only one place you can play that because it's on the "wound third". You can't bend it properly on an acoustic guitar, but you can on an electric. It's the same bend as on AC/DC's "Back in Black", an A bent up to a G. I had to twist my hands into an uncomfortable position and nearly tear the top of my finger off.'

Oblivious to Matthews' contortions, Michael kept on demanding mildly different adaptations of the riff. 'It was really unlike anything else I'd been doing,' says Matthews.

'When I played on Pepsi & Shirlie's "Goodbye Stranger" it was choppy, disco riffing, that rhythmic Nile Rodgers style. But on the "Monkey" tapes, I could already hear some very good rhythm guitar, played by Robert Ahwai. He was the top man, a small guy, very quiet, but a really good player. Also above me in the pecking order were JJ Belle, who contributed some terrific, top-notch guitar to [Grace Jones' Trevor Horn-produced 1985 album] *Slave to the Rhythm*, and of course, Hugh Burns.' Burns had been in the top tier of choices since 'Careless Whisper' in 1984 and had a rich CV. 'Remember, that's Hugh Burns on [Gerry Rafferty's 1978 yacht rock classic] "Baker Street"', says Matthews. 'I think the only reason I got the call to work on "Monkey" was because he was on holiday. Down in fourth place, I just got the shit that was left.'

When *Faith* came out a month or so later, Matthews was surprised to hear himself on the record. 'I didn't think I added much to the tune,' he says, despite his resonant, percussive contribution seeming so integral to the finished article. 'The song was still in fragments, bouncing between two 24-track machines. I don't know whether they did it by recording eight bars, playing the multi-track for eight bars, cutting a section, executing it again, putting it all together on the master. I was just working on little isolated snippets and they joined it together later.' It's all speculation on Matthews' part, but close in spirit to the Porter/Michael working methods we know.

In the UK, 'Monkey''s chart performance was a victim of the diminishing returns suffered by most fifth singles from a particular album, peaking at number 13 in the singles chart.

Not so in America. Sixth single (if we're allowing 'Hard Day''s club release), fourth Hot 100 number one. But it wasn't quite the same version. 'I wasn't that keen on "Monkey" or "Hard Day"', Porter admits now, 'but the remixes were pretty good.' As any producer or lead engineer would, he has mixed feelings about others remixing his work. Still, if it was going to be anyone in the mid- to late 1980s, it may as well have been Jimmy Jam and Terry Lewis (who remixed 'Monkey' for the US number one) and Shep Pettibone (whose remix of 'Hard Day' is an extra track on the original CD and cassette releases of *Faith*). Jam & Lewis brought their trademark robot cowbell, flashes and glissando swoops to 'Monkey' and found room for the song here and there amid the funky debris; Pettibone's beefy 'Hard Day' production is in the vague vicinity of early swingbeat, peppered with karate-chop synths and vocal tomfoolery. Both remixes are 1987/8 in excelsis. 'I was a bit resentful at the time,' says Porter. 'In retrospect, I don't mind at all, providing they do a good job. At that point, Jam & Lewis and Shep Pettibone were at the top of their game – and they probably had teams of people putting this stuff together!' It was a very different situation for Porter, who had assistants in Paul Gomersall and Paul Wright, but was emphatically the man at the controls. Until he fell off a horse, that is. 'I had a terrible accident during the course of making *Faith* – I got thrown off a horse, broke my pelvis and was out of the studio for about two weeks. It was supposed to be six months, but we were right in the middle of it all and there was no way I was going to miss recording the rest of the album. Paul Gomersall took the reins, but George would have been there overseeing it.'

Roddy Matthews was far from excited when he heard the single had been released in America, chiefly because he knew it was a remix. 'I thought, "Oh, that's me fucked then," because I'd had experience of Americans mixing my tracks, and the first thing they'd take off would be what I'd been playing, the Hank Marvin on acid bit, because it's not really helping the rhythm. They'd keep Robert Ahwai's immaculate rhythm playing. I'd had stuff remixed by John "Jellybean" Benitez [producer and remixer, integral to Madonna's early career] and Arthur Baker [electro pioneer, with Afrika Bambaataa and New Order under his belt] and they both picked up on the percussion and rhythmic elements and left out anything else with texture or character. Correctly so, because they were interested in dance mixes.' Well, what do you know? 'When I finally heard the Jam & Lewis remix, I was astonished to find they'd completely removed Ahwai – there's none of his rhythm guitar on it. There's only four people on that [US number one] record and that's George Michael, Jimmy Jam, Terry Lewis and me. That's the company I used to keep.'

Michael pointed out to *No.1* that 'having "a monkey on your back" is American slang for addiction'.[11] Later he'd tell Mark Goodier, 'I'd found out that a girl took some drugs that I didn't know she took; I didn't know how to help her,'[12] so there's a desperation there, an extra angle to a song that's chiefly a statistic now. But what a statistic.

The neurotically focused George Michael was not simply interested in a clean sweep of Hot 100 number one singles, and anyway, he was thwarted from the off when pre-album single 'I Want Your Sex' stalled at number two. Even Michael Jackson couldn't manage it with the contemporaneous *Bad*, although three weeks after 'One More Try' had netted George a commendable hat-trick, Jackson's 'Dirty Diana' cemented the still-standing record (jointly held since 2011 with Katy Perry's *Teenage Dream*) of five US number ones from a single album. George Michael would have to be happy with the extraordinary second place he'd grasped with his mere four after 'Monkey' hit the top. Prince and Madonna weren't even in the contest.

Long before records were set, Michael knew he had achieved one of his most cherished goals. In fact, more than a month before it arrived on American shelves, *Faith* had done exactly what at least some of it was designed to do. 'On "Hard Day" ... the production lacks the balls to make it a creditable dance track,'[13] complained *Record Mirror*'s Eleanor Levy, but a couple of weeks earlier the Shep Pettibone remix, a targeted release in just the United States and Australia, had been pushed out to Black radio and the clubs and duly tore up the *Billboard* Hot Black and Hot Dance charts. In the Hot Black Singles chart it was an eye-catching wildcard, rubbing shoulders with tracks from contemporary stars Shanice Wilson, Alexander O'Neal and Angela Winbush, as well as still-relevant releases from seasoned mainstays Stevie Wonder, Earth, Wind & Fire and, inevitably, Michael Jackson himself. Mission near enough accomplished, and it was only the beginning.

Every week on the various *Billboard* charts seemed to herald a new achievement, most strikingly on the Hot Black Singles and Top Black Albums charts. In April 1988, *Faith* moved up to number three on the Top Black Albums chart, 'the highest ranking for a white act since the Beastie Boys'

Licensed to Ill,[14] before finally claiming the summit on 21 May, 'making him the first white artist to land a No. 1 black album since the Bee Gees scored a decade ago with *Saturday Night Fever*. Michael is the first white *solo* star to ever top the black album chart.'[15] A month on, the ultimate, as *Faith* held on for a fifth week and 'One More Try' made it a double on the Hot Black Singles chart. This time, he was the first white artist to achieve such a feat since funk-rockers Wild Cherry. It would almost be anticlimactic if it wasn't so obviously the culmination of a hard-fought campaign.

Inevitably – understandably – Michael's accomplishments in Black music haven't brought everyone joy. In his essay for *Rock and Popular Music: Politics, Policies, Institutions*, academic and activist Reebee Garofalo bridles at what he sees as *Billboard* Music Editor Nelson George's acquiescence to Michael's 1989 American Music Award for Favorite Soul/R&B Male Artist. 'Not surprisingly,' he writes, 'many African-Americans were offended by what [Nelson] George described as George Michael's "victory". . . . It can perhaps be argued that Michael learned the cultural rules of black music well enough to deliver a performance that was appealing to an African-American audience. But if the "rhythm and blues world", as George puts it, is defined on the basis of shared experience and a common history, then George Michael simply can't be a part of it.'[16]

At least to an extent, Michael realized how contentious his success was. 'He was responsible for me going to *Billboard*,' says Kahane, 'and saying, "George is going to be entering the 'Black' charts and he thinks it's the stupidest name. What, do you have to be black to be on the Black charts?" And they changed it to R&B [in October 1990].' It's a concession of sorts, although the whole exchange smacks of Michael taking the prize without the pushback. He's not appropriating anyone's territory if it's rebranded, is he? Kahane betrays the hard nose behind it all: 'George had a real thing about being the number one artist on the R&B chart.' Another tick in the box.

Signing off

That painstakingly arranged sleeve with its intimate cover shot and self-painted symbols was minutes away from heading out the door. Nothing could go wrong now. 'Back then,' recounts Rob O'Connor, creative director of Stylorouge, 'you would usually do one artwork and forward it to the printer who would make films, duplicate them and send them to various territories around the world. On this occasion, we had to do two artworks – one for London and one for New York – because the States insisted on releasing the album at exactly the same time as the UK.' Of course, the creatives were working up to the wire. 'It was around midnight and we literally had a biker waiting in reception.'

As with any release, it needed a final sign-off from the label. 'You had to photocopy everything in those days,' continues O'Connor, 'and then fax it all off to the record company for proofreading. Once *Faith* was signed off, it was all wrapped up, put in packaging and given to the biker. He promptly got on the M4 motorway [just down the road from Stylorouge's Paddington, West London office] to Heathrow Airport, had an accident and the artwork was wrecked.'

There were unforeseen benefits to *Faith*'s design being so simple; one of them was ease of reproduction. 'As it happens, we'd done some retouching on the image and we had a spare transparency, which was large format, probably 11x14 inches, so we were really lucky. We redid the artwork in the middle of the night and the label ordered another bike. If it had been a really complicated artwork with paintings inside, we would've been screwed.' Kudos to George Michael's steely eyed focus.

Once on the shelves, *Faith* didn't stay long. According to Mark Goodier in his interview with Michael for 2011's *Faith: Legacy Edition* deluxe reissue, the album sold one million copies in the United States in its first week of release alone ('Really?'[1] was Michael's response). The stranglehold it put on the *Billboard* charts was absolute, a cumulative twelve weeks at number one on Top Pop Albums, four weeks on top of the Hot 100 for 'Faith', two for 'Father Figure', three for 'One More Try', two for 'Monkey' and then – as we've seen – there were the unprecedented displays on the Black charts, plus twelve months' presence on Hot Crossover, Hot Adult Contemporary and healthy showings on the Club Play and 12-Inch Singles Sales charts. Unusually, back home in the UK, there was just one week at number one on the Top 100 Albums and none for any of the singles. Michael initially blamed an abiding 'tabloid image which is really strong in England',[2] but was probably closer to the mark identifying a 'stigma. I've never been keen on the idea of having to sell myself as an adult. As I say, in America it hasn't been necessary. I'm accepted as an adult because the music has already done it.'[3] The adult audiences of Britain were still hung up on the George Michael of Wham! – and wouldn't really take him to their hearts until the refinements of 1996's *Older* – but the pop mags had ditched him. By mid-1988, *Smash Hits* was all Kylie Minogue and Bros, and Michael was the boring 'glummest man in pop'. In a pocket-sized profile of Deon Estus, the bassist is said to only sleep 'for two hours every night (probably when he's on stage with George ho ho)'.[4]

Michael could comfort himself with ludicrous global sales and the vastly successful *Faith* tour that began at Tokyo's Budokan on 19 February 1988 and finished at Florida's Pensacola Civic Center on 31 October the same year (with a small Spanish addendum the following summer), boosting the album further into the stratosphere. Somehow none of it was the solace it should have been, because Michael was starting to realize two salient facts: he didn't like touring and he didn't want to be famous.

'I hate being on tour,' he told *US Weekly* a third of the way through the actual tour, 'because you're surrounded by your own public persona twenty-four hours a day.'[5] 'I hate the actual traveling, but I like playing,' he clarified to *Interview* magazine. 'I'm discovering problems in performing for a George Michael audience, because I'm 25 years old, and for five years I have written in a style that's appealed to people who are either older or younger than me. This tour is really the climax of that problem because 50 percent of the people I perform for have come to scream at me and the other 50 percent have come to listen to the music.'[6] In that sense, the album that was supposed to make the leap ends up transitional. The *Rolling Stone* review of the tour's first US date at Landover's Capital Centre on 6 August noted, 'adoring masses, which included a healthy percentage of mother-daughter teams' with the 'remarkable singer and pop songsmith'[7] bridging the divide.

As far back as March 1985, Michael was admitting, 'I don't think I can face another year of [fame],'[8] but ambition trumped self-preservation. Looking back on 1988, having decompressed, he told *Q*, 'As far as stardom in America is concerned, you only make that first impression once, as a solo artist; you only have that big, big year once. And that's all I need . . . fame can't do anything else for me.'[9]

If *Faith* was tight, what followed was looser, the focus shifting. '*Faith* did more than 10 million sales in the United States and has a Diamond certification,' says Paul Gambaccini. 'You don't get many of those anymore. So, who would have believed that it could all go away so fast?' Nobody but George. His retreat into relative obscurity, sinking deeper into his leather jacket until he was out of the frame altogether – drolly replaced by Linda Evangelista, Cindy Crawford, Naomi Campbell and the rest of fashion's pantheon of supermodels in the 'Freedom 90' video, letting that leather burn – was a jarring reaction to his ubiquity in the *Faith* era. Michael had achieved what he set out to do and didn't like it half as much as he expected. He was briefly the most bankable (white) pop star in the world, but didn't want to be a commodity anymore.

Gambaccini has a take that's rather more personal. 'Part of it was because he wanted to be a very private gay man,' he suggests. Michael wouldn't meet his first real love, Anselmo Feleppa, until January 1991 at the Rock in Rio festival in Brazil. That relationship and Feleppa's tragic death on 26 March 1993 does, of course, at least partly explain the lengthier hiatus between *Listen Without Prejudice Vol. 1* and *Older*, but perhaps Michael's earlier relationship with photographer Brad Branson is the precursor – and a similar distraction at the end of the 1980s. What his friends and collaborators recognize now is a miasma of loneliness. 'He was clearly more troubled than someone like me realized,' says Steve Sidwell 'and I worked with him sporadically for more than 30 years.' 'I met him and Chris [Porter] in Sarm West Studio 2 after *Faith*,' says Andy Duncan. 'I remember looking at George staring back at me, and I sensed this feeling of isolation. I wouldn't cherish that level of success, where other people think they own you.' It's the emotional futility of the exercise that pulls you up short. As Michael told John Aizlewood of *Q* in an intensely raw interview ten years after the album, 'I wanted to compete with Michael Jackson and Madonna and did everything I could to get there. I was 24 and thought, "Fuck, this isn't very much fun." I was at an incredible low. I was so lonely. . . . I was chasing the wrong things to be happy.'[10]

'We could've kept going,' says Rob Kahane. 'We just decided that enough was enough. It was, like, two straight years of George Michael on the radio, so we had to stop for a while.' It soon turned out 'a while' wouldn't suffice. Michael wanted to turn the tap off permanently. 'We'd spent all this time creating this George Michael character – because he never considered that to be him – and he just felt that it had gone too far.' As the man employed to make that character as popular as humanly possible, Kahane struggled to understand the effect on his boss's psyche. 'I was trying to get inside his head. He was retreating because of his personal life.'

Michael had built the image, now he was tearing it down. He'd wrestled with status anxiety, and now he wanted rid of any status at all. The Grammy for Album of the Year, those controversial American Music Awards, the Brits, the Ivor Novello, the millions of albums still pouring out of the stores – that could all stay in the one big year. 'After *Faith*, he'd dominated the 1980s in America as a British male,' says Gambaccini, 'and he was poised to dominate the 1990s.' Instead, he began them with hundreds of anonymous faces – and certainly not his own – on the *Listen Without Prejudice Vol. 1* cover, a simple lyric video for 'Praying for Time' and a manager wondering why he was still there. 'I had to go to the record company and tell them, "Hey, he doesn't want to do any publicity, no interviews, no touring, no nothing,"' says Kahane. 'And they were saying, "Well, what are we supposed to do?"'

Faith hadn't been named for religion – after all, he differentiates between the two in the symbols on the cover – but for his renewed trust in the music business ('I've come through that period, better than I thought I would, and it's given me optimism and faith'[11]) and now he was shunning it again. He'd taken aim at the triple crown, effected the perfect crossover move, cut links with the past and produced songs for posterity, and now he'd wiped himself out. 'Doing a George Michael.' It's harder than it looks.

Notes

Unless noted, all quotes are from interviews conducted by the author between March and July 2021.

Wham! wrapped

1 Bitz, 'A Letter from George Michael', *Smash Hits*, 4 June 1986. Emphasis in original.

2 Alexandra Topping, 'The Philanthropic Acts of George Michael: From £5K Tips to Nurses' Gigs', *The Guardian*, 26 December 2016.

3 Ian Birch, 'Wham!: The Sundance Kids', *Smash Hits*, 18 August 1983.

4 Andrew Ridgeley, *Wham! George & Me* (London: Michael Joseph, 2019).

5 Peter Martin, 'Andrew Knew He Was There for a Purpose', *Smash Hits*, 18 June 1986.

6 Rob Tannenbaum, 'George Michael: Artist or Airhead?', *Musician*, January 1988.

7 Dave Rimmer, 'You Don't Have to Say You Love Him: The Divine Simon Napier-Bell', *Q*, April 1987.

8 Adrian Deevoy, '1988: George Michael', *Q*, January 1990.

The public image

1 Orla Brennan, 'Peter Saville, Interviewed by Our Readers', *AnOther Magazine*, 20 April 2020.

2 Steve Sutherland, 'Blind Faith', *Melody Maker*, 7 November 1987.

3 Jon Bowermaster, 'Michael Unmasked', *Chicago Tribune*, 4 September 1988.

4 Stephen Holden, 'RECORDINGS: George Michael on Fame and "Freedom"', *New York Times*, 16 September 1990.

5 'Personal File: Boy George', *Smash Hits*, 16 December 1987.

6 Susan Rozsnyai, 'George Michael's Cousin and Confidant Andreas Georgiou Shares Family Photos and Talks Openly of Their Life Together and the Star's Recent Traumas', *Hello!*, 24 October 1998.

7 Showbiz Team: Sean Hoare and James Scott, 'Cousin Walks Out on Cocky George – Bust-Up over Arrest', *The Sun*, November 1998.

8 Ridgeley, *Wham! George & Me*.

9 Judy Wieder, 'George Michael: All the Way Out', *The Advocate*, 19 January 1999.

10 'Jonathan Ross and George Michael Have Words', [TV Programme] Channel 4, 19 June 1987.

11 Sylvia Patterson, 'The Glummest Man in Pop?', *Smash Hits*, 18 November 1987. Emphasis in original.

12 Debbi Voller, 'The Last Wham! Interview EVER', *No.1*, 28 June 1986.

Freedom 87

1 Simon Napier-Bell, *I'm Coming to Take You to Lunch* (London: Ebury Press, 2005).

2 Mark Goodier, 'Spring 2010: With George Michael', *Faith: Legacy Edition*, Sony Music, 2011.

3 Alan Jackson, 'Tart with a Heart', *NME*, 20 June 1987.

4 George Michael and Tony Parsons, *Bare* (London: Michael Joseph, 1990).

5 Ibid.

6 Ibid.

7 Andrew Brel, 'An Affair of the Craft', *Guitarist*, January 2002.

8 Craig Rosen, *The Billboard Book of Number One Albums: The Inside Story behind Pop Music's Blockbuster Records* (New York: Billboard Books, 1996).

9 'Video Killed the Radio Star – The Directors View: Andy Morahan', [TV Programme] 3DD Productions, 9 June 2009.

10 Lola Borg, 'Review: Singles', *Smash Hits*, 7 October 1987.

11 Sean O'Hagan, '45', *NME*, 17 October 1987.

12 'Video Killed the Radio Star – The Directors View: Andy Morahan', 2009.

Sex and the serious man

1 Adam Sweeting, 'Tears For Fears: Talking in Riddles', *Melody Maker*, 26 November 1983.

2 'But How Did They Vote?', *Smash Hits*, 18 December 1985.

3 Adrian Deevoy, 'George Michael: The Lone Star State', *Q*, June 1988.

4 Tannenbaum, 'George Michael: Artist or Airhead?'.

5 'Jonathan Ross and George Michael Have Words', 1987.

6 *Melody Maker*, 6 June 1987.

7 Eleanor Levy, 'There's a Lot of Paranoia Involved with Being Famous', *Record Mirror*, 20 June 1987.

8 Barry McIlheney, 'Review: Singles', *Smash Hits*, 20 May 1987.

9 Michele Kirsch, '45', *NME*, 6 June 1987.

10 Lesley O'Toole, 'Singles', *Record Mirror*, 13 June 1987.

11 Kerryn Ramsey, 'I Was an Arrogant, Narcissistic Egomaniac', *Looks*, November 1990.

12 Richard Buskin, 'Classic Tracks: George Michael "Faith"', *Sound on Sound*, March 2013.

13 Ibid.

14 Richard Smith and Steve Pafford, 'George Talks: His Frankest Interview Ever', *Gay Times*, July 2007.

15 Danny Kelly, 'Idoling Away the Years', *NME*, 16 November 1985.

16 Chris Heath, 'George Michael: Love, Sex and Stupid Wigs', *Smash Hits*, 3 June 1987.

17 Wieder, 'George Michael'.

18 Smith and Pafford, 'George Talks'.

19 Kim Freeman, 'Stations Want Love, Not Sex', *Billboard*, 27 June 1987.

20 Adam Sweeting, 'By George, He's Really Got It', *The Guardian*, 9 November 1987.

Politics (the pop remix)

1 'Boy's Back', *Melody Maker*, 17 January 1987.

2 Rob Jovanovic, *George Michael: The Biography 1963–2016* (London: Piatkus Books, 2017).

3 'Two New Bands Rise from Dexys & Wham!', *Melody Maker*, 22 October 1983.

4 'Mutterings', *Smash Hits*, 29 September 1983.

5 'Two New Bands Rise From Dexys & Wham!'.

6 Ibid.

7 David Fricke, 'The Second Coming of George Michael', *Rolling Stone*, 20 November 1986.

8 Sutherland, 'Blind Faith'.

9 Paul Simper, 'Faith: GM Speaks', *No.1*, 14 November 1987.

10 Ibid.

11 Ibid.

12 Goodier, 'Spring 2010'.

13 Paul Simper, 'Wham! Bam! I Am!', *Melody Maker*, 30 October 1982.

14 Adrian Thrills, 'Wham!', *NME*, 19 June 1982.

15 Dave McCullough, 'The Odd Couple', *Sounds*, 8 October 1983.

16 Nick Kent, 'Slag! Miners' Benefit Finale, London Royal Festival Hall', *NME*, 22 September 1984.

17 Ibid.

18 Adam Sweeting, 'Pit-Head Ballet: Wham!/Style Council, Miners' Benefit, Royal Festival Hall, London', *Melody Maker*, 15 September 1984.

19 Colin Irwin, 'Wham!: The Bigger They Come, the Harder They Bite', *Melody Maker*, 17 November 1984.

20 Tannenbaum, 'George Michael'.

21 Ian Birch, 'Wham! Make It Bigger', *Smash Hits*, 27 September 1984.

22 Irwin, 'Wham!: The Bigger They Come, the Harder They Bite'.

23 Topping, 'The Philanthropic Acts of George Michael'.

24 Liz Nickson, 'George Michael', *Life*, September 1988.

25 Stuart Maconie and David Quantick, 'The Strongest Day', *NME*, 18 June 1988.

26 Levy, 'There's a Lot of Paranoia'.

27 Richard Cook, 'Songs Sung Blue', *Sounds*, 7 November 1987.

28 Myrna Minkoff, 'George, Best', *NME*, 7 November 1987.

29 Eleanor Levy, 'Albums', *Record Mirror*, 7 November 1987. Emphasis in original.

30 Steve Pond, 'George Michael, Seriously', *Rolling Stone*, 28 January 1988.

I will be your adult contemporary

1 David Jensen, 'Everything He Wants', *No.1*, 21 February 1987.

2 Heath, 'George Michael'.

3 Chi Ming Lai, 'ALISON MOYET Interview', *Electricity Club*, 10 June 2013.

4 Simper, 'Faith: GM Speaks'.

5 Chris Heath, 'Uneven', *Q*, December 1987.

6 'Album Reviews: Spotlight', *Billboard*, 14 November 1987.

7 Simper, 'Faith: GM Speaks'.

8 Jane Moore, 'George Michael on Beating Drugs, Depression and His Outing in LA', *GQ*, October 2004.

9 'Georgie Boy', *Melody Maker*, 16 January 1988.

10 Andy Morahan, 'What I Wish I'd Known and a Few Other Things I've Learnt along the Way', *Young Director Award*, 27 January 2010.

Bearing the crossover

1 Simper, 'Faith: GM Speaks'.

2 Tony Parsons, 'Tales from the Gymnasium', *The Face*, November 1987.

3 Napier-Bell, *I'm Coming to Take You to Lunch*.

4 Peter Martin, 'A Year in the Life of Wham! As Told by George Michael', *The Smash Hits Yearbook 1986*, December 1986.

5 Nickson, 'George Michael'.

6 'The Faith Tour: Selected Interview Clips', [TV Programme] MTV, 2 February 1988.

7 Jessica Goodman and Kevin O'Donnell, 'Remembering George Michael: Friends and Collaborators Pay Tribute', *Entertainment Weekly*, 4 January 2017.

8 Brad Balfour, 'George Michael Wants Your Respect', *Spin*, December 1987.

9 Ibid.

10 Michael Goldberg, 'Cameo's Black-Rock Breakthrough', *Rolling Stone*, 15 January 1987.

11 Simper, 'Faith: GM Speaks'.

12 Goodier, 'Spring 2010'.

13 Eleanor Levy, 'Albums', *Record Mirror*, 7 November 1987.

14 Paul Grein, 'Chart Beat', *Billboard*, 16 April 1988.

15 Paul Grein, 'Chart Beat', *Billboard*, 21 May 1988.

16 Reebee Garofalo, 'Black Popular Music: Crossing Over or Going Under', in *Rock and Popular Music: Politics, Policies, Institutions*, ed. Tony Bennett, Simon Frith, Lawrence Grossberg, John Shepherd and Graeme Turner (London: Routledge, 1993), pp. 234, 237.

Signing off

1 Goodier, 'Spring 2010'.

2 Paul Simper, 'My Advice to Bros . . .', *No.1*, 30 April 1988.

3 Deevoy, 'George Michael: The Lone Star State'.

4 Bitz, 'This Man "Hangs Out" with the Glummest Man in Pop!', *Smash Hits*, 13 July 1988.

5 Jon Bowermaster, 'Act of Faith', *US Weekly*, 30 May 1988.

6 Joseph Perkins, 'Souled Out: George Michael', *Interview*, October 1988.

7 David Wild, ' "Faith" in the Flesh', *Rolling Stone*, 22 September 1988.

8 David Thomas, 'Wham: Why We've Reached Breaking Point', *No.1*, 9 March 1985.

9 Deevoy, '1988: George Michael'.

10 John Aizlewood, 'I Am What I Am', *Q*, December 1998.

11 Simon Mills, 'George Michael: No Sex Please', *Sky*, 22 October 1987.

Selected bibliography

Bennett, Tony, Simon Frith, Lawrence Grossberg, John Shepherd and Graeme Turner, *Rock and Popular Music: Politics, Policies, Institutions*. London: Routledge, 1993.

Herbert, Emily, *George Michael: The Life 1963–2016*. London: John Blake, 2017.

Jones, Dylan, *Sweet Dreams: The Story of the New Romantics*. London: Faber & Faber, 2020.

Jovanovic, Rob, *George Michael: The Biography 1963–2016*. London: Piatkus Books, 2017.

Marsh, Dave, *The Heart of Rock and Soul: The 1001 Greatest Singles Ever Made*. London: Penguin, 1989.

Michael, George, and Tony Parsons, *Bare*. London: Michael Joseph, 1990.

Napier-Bell, Simon, *Black Vinyl, White Powder*. London: Ebury Press, 2002.

Napier-Bell, Simon, *I'm Coming to Take You to Lunch*. London: Ebury Press, 2005.

Ridgeley, Andrew, *Wham! George & Me*. London: Michael Joseph, 2019.

Ross, Alex, *The Rest Is Noise*. London: Harper Perennial, 2009.

Smith, Sean, *George*. London: HarperCollins, 2017.

Stanley, Bob, *Yeah Yeah Yeah: The Story of Modern Pop*. London: Faber & Faber, 2013.

Steele, Robert, *Careless Whispers: The Life & Career of George Michael*. London: Omnibus Press, 2011.

1. *Dusty Springfield's Dusty in Memphis* by Warren Zanes
2. *Love's Forever Changes* by Andrew Hultkrans
3. *Neil Young's Harvest* by Sam Inglis
4. *The Kinks' The Kinks Are the Village Green Preservation Society* by Andy Miller
5. *The Smiths' Meat Is Murder* by Joe Pernice
6. *Pink Floyd's The Piper at the Gates of Dawn* by John Cavanagh
7. *ABBA's ABBA Gold: Greatest Hits* by Elisabeth Vincentelli
8. *The Jimi Hendrix Experience's Electric Ladyland* by John Perry
9. *Joy Division's Unknown Pleasures* by Chris Ott
10. *Prince's Sign "☉" the Times* by Michaelangelo Matos
11. *The Velvet Underground's The Velvet Underground & Nico* by Joe Harvard
12. *The Beatles' Let It Be* by Steve Matteo
13. *James Brown's Live at the Apollo* by Douglas Wolk
14. *Jethro Tull's Aqualung* by Allan Moore
15. *Radiohead's OK Computer* by Dai Griffiths
16. *The Replacements' Let It Be* by Colin Meloy
17. *Led Zeppelin's Led Zeppelin IV* by Erik Davis
18. *The Rolling Stones' Exile on Main St.* by Bill Janovitz
19. *The Beach Boys' Pet Sounds* by Jim Fusilli
20. *Ramones' Ramones* by Nicholas Rombes
21. *Elvis Costello's Armed Forces* by Franklin Bruno
22. *R.E.M.'s Murmur* by J. Niimi
23. *Jeff Buckley's Grace* by Daphne Brooks
24. *DJ Shadow's Endtroducing...* by Eliot Wilder
25. *MC5's Kick Out the Jams* by Don McLeese
26. *David Bowie's Low* by Hugo Wilcken

27. *Bruce Springsteen's Born in the U.S.A.* by Geoffrey Himes

28. *The Band's Music from Big Pink* by John Niven

29. *Neutral Milk Hotel's In the Aeroplane over the Sea* by Kim Cooper

30. *Beastie Boys' Paul's Boutique* by Dan Le Roy

31. *Pixies' Doolittle* by Ben Sisario

32. *Sly and the Family Stone's There's a Riot Goin' On* by Miles Marshall Lewis

33. *The Stone Roses' The Stone Roses* by Alex Green

34. *Nirvana's In Utero* by Gillian G. Gaar

35. *Bob Dylan's Highway 61 Revisited* by Mark Polizzotti

36. *My Bloody Valentine's Loveless* by Mike McGonigal

37. *The Who's The Who Sell Out* by John Dougan

38. *Guided by Voices' Bee Thousand* by Marc Woodworth

39. *Sonic Youth's Daydream Nation* by Matthew Stearns

40. *Joni Mitchell's Court and Spark* by Sean Nelson

41. *Guns N' Roses' Use Your Illusion I and II* by Eric Weisbard

42. *Stevie Wonder's Songs in the Key of Life* by Zeth Lundy

43. *The Byrds' The Notorious Byrd Brothers* by Ric Menck

44. *Captain Beefheart's Trout Mask Replica* by Kevin Courrier

45. *Minutemen's Double Nickels on the Dime* by Michael T. Fournier

46. *Steely Dan's Aja* by Don Breithaupt

47. *A Tribe Called Quest's People's Instinctive Travels and the Paths of Rhythm* by Shawn Taylor

48. *PJ Harvey's Rid of Me* by Kate Schatz

49. *U2's Achtung Baby* by Stephen Catanzarite

50. *Belle & Sebastian's If You're Feeling Sinister* by Scott Plagenhoef

51. *Nick Drake's Pink Moon* by Amanda Petrusich

52. *Celine Dion's Let's Talk About Love* by Carl Wilson

53. *Tom Waits' Swordfishtrombones* by David Smay

54. *Throbbing Gristle's 20 Jazz Funk Greats* by Drew Daniel

55. *Patti Smith's Horses* by Philip Shaw

56. *Black Sabbath's Master of Reality* by John Darnielle

57. *Slayer's Reign in Blood* by D. X. Ferris

58. *Richard and Linda Thompson's Shoot Out the Lights* by Hayden Childs

59. *The Afghan Whigs' Gentlemen* by Bob Gendron

60. *The Pogues' Rum, Sodomy, and the Lash* by Jeffery T. Roesgen

61. *The Flying Burrito Brothers' The Gilded Palace of Sin* by Bob Proehl

62. *Wire's Pink Flag* by Wilson Neate

63. *Elliott Smith's XO* by Mathew Lemay

64. *Nas' Illmatic* by Matthew Gasteier

65. *Big Star's Radio City* by Bruce Eaton

66. *Madness' One Step Beyond. . .* by Terry Edwards

67. *Brian Eno's Another Green World* by Geeta Dayal

68. *The Flaming Lips' Zaireeka* by Mark Richardson

69. *The Magnetic Fields' 69 Love Songs* by LD Beghtol

70. *Israel Kamakawiwo'ole's Facing Future* by Dan Kois

71. *Public Enemy's It Takes a Nation of Millions to Hold Us Back* by Christopher R. Weingarten

72. *Pavement's Wowee Zowee* by Bryan Charles

73. *AC/DC's Highway to Hell* by Joe Bonomo

74. *Van Dyke Parks's Song Cycle* by Richard Henderson

75. *Slint's Spiderland* by Scott Tennent

76. *Radiohead's Kid A* by Marvin Lin

77. *Fleetwood Mac's Tusk* by Rob Trucks

78. *Nine Inch Nails' Pretty Hate Machine* by Daphne Carr

79. *Ween's Chocolate and Cheese* by Hank Shteamer

80. *Johnny Cash's American Recordings* by Tony Tost

81. *The Rolling Stones' Some Girls* by Cyrus Patell

82. *Dinosaur Jr.'s You're Living All Over Me* by Nick Attfield

83. *Television's Marquee Moon* by Bryan Waterman

84. *Aretha Franklin's Amazing Grace* by Aaron Cohen

85. *Portishead's Dummy* by RJ Wheaton

86. *Talking Heads' Fear of Music* by Jonathan Lethem

87. *Serge Gainsbourg's Histoire de Melody Nelson* by Darran Anderson

88. *They Might Be Giants' Flood* by S. Alexander Reed and Elizabeth Sandifer

89. *Andrew W.K.'s I Get Wet* by Phillip Crandall

90. *Aphex Twin's Selected Ambient Works Volume II* by Marc Weidenbaum

91. *Gang of Four's Entertainment* by Kevin J. H. Dettmar

92. *Richard Hell and the Voidoids' Blank Generation* by Pete Astor

93. *J Dilla's Donuts* by Jordan Ferguson

94. *The Beach Boys' Smile* by Luis Sanchez

95. *Oasis' Definitely Maybe* by Alex Niven

96. *Liz Phair's Exile in Guyville* by Gina Arnold

97. *Kanye West's My Beautiful Dark Twisted Fantasy* by Kirk Walker Graves

98. *Danger Mouse's The Grey Album* by Charles Fairchild

99. *Sigur Rós's ()* by Ethan Hayden

100. *Michael Jackson's Dangerous* by Susan Fast

101. *Can's Tago Mago* by Alan Warner

102. *Bobbie Gentry's Ode to Billie Joe* by Tara Murtha

103. *Hole's Live Through This* by Anwen Crawford

104. *Devo's Freedom of Choice* by Evie Nagy

105. *Dead Kennedys' Fresh Fruit for Rotting Vegetables* by Michael Stewart Foley

106. *Koji Kondo's Super Mario Bros.* by Andrew Schartmann

107. *Beat Happening's Beat Happening* by Bryan C. Parker

108. *Metallica's Metallica* by David Masciotra

109. *Phish's A Live One* by Walter Holland

110. *Miles Davis' Bitches Brew* by George Grella Jr.

111. *Blondie's Parallel Lines* by Kembrew McLeod

112. *Grateful Dead's Workingman's Dead* by Buzz Poole

113. *New Kids On The Block's Hangin' Tough* by Rebecca Wallwork

114. *The Geto Boys' The Geto Boys* by Rolf Potts

115. *Sleater-Kinney's Dig Me Out* by Jovana Babovic

116. *LCD Soundsystem's Sound of Silver* by Ryan Leas

117. *Donny Hathaway's Donny Hathaway Live* by Emily J. Lordi

118. *The Jesus and Mary Chain's Psychocandy* by Paula Mejia

119. *The Modern Lovers' The Modern Lovers* by Sean L. Maloney

120. *Angelo Badalamenti's Soundtrack from Twin Peaks* by Clare Nina Norelli

121. *Young Marble Giants' Colossal Youth* by Michael Blair and Joe Bucciero

122. *The Pharcyde's Bizarre Ride II the Pharcyde* by Andrew Barker

123. *Arcade Fire's The Suburbs* by Eric Eidelstein

124. *Bob Mould's Workbook* by Walter Biggins and Daniel Couch

125. *Camp Lo's Uptown Saturday Night* by Patrick Rivers and Will Fulton

126. *The Raincoats' The Raincoats* by Jenn Pelly

127. *Björk's Homogenic* by Emily Mackay

128. *Merle Haggard's Okie from Muskogee* by Rachel Lee Rubin

129. *Fugazi's In on the Kill Taker* by Joe Gross

130. *Jawbreaker's 24 Hour Revenge Therapy* by Ronen Givony

131. *Lou Reed's Transformer* by Ezra Furman

132. *Siouxsie and the Banshees' Peepshow* by Samantha Bennett

133. *Drive-By Truckers' Southern Rock Opera* by Rien Fertel

134. *dc Talk's Jesus Freak* by Will Stockton and D. Gilson

135. *Tori Amos's Boys for Pele* by Amy Gentry

136. *Odetta's One Grain of Sand* by Matthew Frye Jacobson

137. *Manic Street Preachers' The Holy Bible* by David Evans

138. *The Shangri-Las' Golden Hits of the Shangri-Las* by Ada Wolin

139. *Tom Petty's Southern Accents* by Michael Washburn

140. *Massive Attack's Blue Lines* by Ian Bourland

141. *Wendy Carlos's Switched-On Bach* by Roshanak Kheshti

142. *The Wild Tchoupitoulas' The Wild Tchoupitoulas* by Bryan Wagner

143. *David Bowie's Diamond Dogs* by Glenn Hendler

144. *D'Angelo's Voodoo* by Faith A. Pennick

145. *Judy Garland's Judy at Carnegie Hall* by Manuel Betancourt

146. *Elton John's Blue Moves* by Matthew Restall

147. *Various Artists' I'm Your Fan: The Songs of Leonard Cohen* by Ray Padgett

148. *Janet Jackson's The Velvet Rope* by Ayanna Dozier

149. *Suicide's Suicide* by Andi Coulter

150. *Elvis Presley's From Elvis in Memphis* by Eric Wolfson

151. *Nick Cave and the Bad Seeds' Murder Ballads* by Santi Elijah Holley

152. *24 Carat Black's Ghetto: Misfortune's Wealth* by Zach Schonfeld

153. *Carole King's Tapestry* by Loren Glass

154. *Pearl Jam's Vs.* by Clint Brownlee

155. *Roxy Music's Avalon* by Simon Morrison

156. *Duran Duran's Rio* by Annie Zaleski

157. *Donna Summer's Once Upon a Time* by Alex Jeffery

158. *Sam Cooke's Live at the Harlem Square Club, 1963* by Colin Fleming

159. *Janelle Monáe's The ArchAndroid* by Alyssa Favreau

160. *John Prine's John Prine* by Erin Osmon

161. *Maria Callas's Lyric and Coloratura Arias* by Ginger Dellenbaugh

162. *The National's Boxer* by Ryan Pinkard

163. *Kraftwerk's Computer World* by Steve Tupai Francis

164. *Cat Power's Moon Pix* by Donna Kozloskie

165. *George Michael's Faith* by Matthew Horton